# Whatever You Do
## for the
## Least of These

# Whatever You Do for the Least of These

Pat Fosarelli

Liguori
LIGUORI, MISSOURI

*Imprimi Potest:*
Richard Thibodeau, C.Ss.R.
Provincial, Denver Province
The Redemptorists

Published by Liguori Publications
Liguori, Missouri
www.liguori.org
www.catholicbooksonline.com

**Library of Congress Cataloging-in-Publication Data**

Fosarelli, Patricia Diane.
    Whatever you do for the least of these : ministering to ill and dying children and their families / Patricia Fosarelli.— 1st ed.
      p. cm.
    ISBN 0-7648-0984-9 (pbk.)
    1. Church work with sick children. I. Title.

BV4335 .F67 2003
259'.41'083—dc21                        2002023976

Scripture quotations are taken from the *New Revised Standard Version Bible*, copyright 1989 by the Division of Christian Education of the National Council of the Churches of Christ in the U.S.A. Used by permission. All rights reserved.

Printed in the United States of America
07 06 05 04 03  5 4 3 2 1
First edition

*To all the ill children
and their families whom I have served
in pediatrics and ministry.*

# Contents

# Introduction

## Why Is There a Need
## for a Book of This Type?

In my experience as a pediatrician, I have been with many ill and dying children and their parents. Often, I am in the hospital room just as a pastoral visitor (ordained or lay) enters. All too often, the visitor greets parents and child upon entering, but then almost always turns his or her attention exclusively to the adults in the room, even though it is the child who is ill.

For infants and toddlers, this does not usually present any problems, but that is not true for school-age children and adolescents. These young people feel that they are being ignored while the visitor talks to the "important" people—their parents. Perfectly capable of expressing their own feelings, such children and adolescents frequently retreat into stony silence when the visitor finally turns his or her attention back to them. As one child said to me, "I hate when people say they're coming to see me, but they only want to talk to my mom when they're here." Or as an eleven-year-old boy screamed, "I'm the one who's sick! Why won't people even look at me? Do I look that ugly?"

Most adults, of course, do not mean to ignore the ill

child or adolescent; they simply are at a loss for words or appropriate action. After all, what are the proper words to say to a newly paralyzed ten-year-old? What is the most appropriate pastoral comment that one can make to a dying eight-year-old? Unfortunately, most of our schools of theology and seminaries do not teach classes on communication skills with children even under the best of circumstances, let alone times of catastrophic illness or injury. Many visitors who are themselves parents rely on their own experiences, but this may be limited to the age and gender of their own children. Other lay visitors have never had children of their own or have had extremely limited contact with children.

Furthermore, many visitors react to an ill, injured, or dying child or teen as they would react to their own child or teen in that same situation. This is a very natural response. Loving parents and relatives of children and adolescents care deeply about them. The thought of anything terrible happening to them evokes a deep-seated, gut-wrenching response. This is especially true if the child or teen is similar in age, gender, appearance, or mannerisms to one's own beloved child or teen.

I believe that I can make a contribution with this book. I have been a pediatrician for a quarter of a century and have taken care of many seriously or chronically ill children and adolescents in my career. I have been at the bedsides of dying children as they made the transition from this life to the next. Furthermore, my doctoral work in ministry, on the spiritual development of children in health and disease, permits me to bridge the physical, emotional, and spiritual worlds of ill or dying children and their families.

I come to you as one who has had to break very bad news of terminal conditions to parents and children alike. I come to you as one who has held the hands of parents as they watched their child's life ebbing away. I come to you as one who has been at the bedside of dying children and adolescents when their parents were absent.

No death is ever easy. Even though my faith assures me that the person who is dying is moving to a better life, the loss of a child or adolescent as a person on earth, a member of someone's family and our society, hurts. The death of one's child or adolescent violates the human view of the natural order of things, namely, that the oldest die first and the youngest last.

Simply stated, there is a need for a book of this type because there is so very little available for pastoral visitors (ordained or lay) who may be called to represent their churches at the bedsides of children and adolescents. We are called to minister to our brothers and sisters in need, even the youngest. We do not minister most effectively if we cannot meet children and their families "where they are." To do that well, we need to know something about emotional and spiritual developmental stages of children (and their families) in health and disease. The chapters in this book focus on the various developmental stages at each age, because these need to be well understood. It can be embarrassing for a pastoral visitor and humiliating or confusing for a child or teen when expectations of development do not match reality.

This book is not intended to make anyone an expert in child development and family dynamics. Only long study, direct experience with children and their families, and the grace of God can bring one to a place of proficiency. That said, this book will introduce pastoral visitors to the main issues confronting children of different ages and adolescents when they are faced with illness, injury, or dying. Furthermore, it will highlight the issues faced by their parents and their siblings in these same circumstances. It will offer advice on what a pastoral visitor can do and what he or she should not do. It will offer suggestions for prayers or services, depending on the child's developmental level and family's needs.

# Theodicy Issues

Working with children and adolescents (and their families) who are facing seemingly insurmountable challenges in terms of illness and catastrophic injury always seems to bring certain theological issues to the foreground. Most notable are issues of theodicy—or why God lets evil exist. *Why does God permit children and adolescents to suffer?* Indeed, this very question, at the onset of my own medical career, left me so confused and angry that I did not go to church for nine years. As I watched children and adolescents die, beautiful human beings (some of whom were not that much younger than I was at the time), I wondered who and where God was in the midst of all this misery.

This is not a new question for humankind. We read of the question being asked in various world scriptures, as well as throughout human history, especially during plagues, wars, and famine. The question has been asked, in various ways, in great fiction as well. Perhaps one of the best known appears in Dostoevsky's *The Brothers Karamazov*. In the chapter "Rebellion," the cynical Ivan is having an intense discussion with his saintly brother Alyosha about the ugliness of human nature. After giving several examples of horrific deeds against children, he says:

> But then what about the children, what shall I do about them? That's the question I cannot answer. For the hundredth time, I repeat—the questions are endless, but I am only considering the children because in their case what I have to say is incontrovertibly clear. Listen: if everyone has to suffer to bring about eternal harmony through that suffering, tell me, please, what have children to do with this? It's quite incomprehensible that they too should have to suffer, that they too should have to pay for harmony by their suffering. Why should they be the grist to someone else's mill, the means of ensuring someone's future harmony? (...) [T]herefore I absolutely reject that higher harmony. It's not worth one little tear from one single little tortured child....

As a young, newly graduated physician, I, like Ivan, was deeply troubled and said to myself repeatedly, "If I can see that the suffering of children is wrong, and if I knew that if I had the power to bring it all to an end, even I would do so. So, why doesn't God do something? After all, God is all-powerful and all-merciful, and I surely am not. Yet, I can see what needs to be done. Where is God? Who is this God?"

It would be an understatement to say that this issue brought me pain. Always a very spiritual child, I grew up with the idea that God loved me, and God wanted what was good for me. Furthermore, I believed that God loved all persons and wanted what was in their best interests as well. The crisis that I experienced in medical school as I watched unsuccessful resuscitations of children battered by their parents, the tortured lives of very premature infants who struggled to take their next breaths, and the immeasurable suffering endured by children because of malignancies and the medications or therapies to combat them shook the very core of my being. If I could be so moved, why wasn't God? I used to say to a God in whom I wasn't sure I believed, "Fix it, will you?"

I am much older now. I still don't have the answer as to why God permits the suffering of children (or any human being for that matter). Although I don't now *need* the answer, I still wish that I could make suffering go away. Over the years, I learned that I could not expect God to appear like some genie and correct each and every situation. I came to understand that, on some level, *my* presence was God's answer to people's prayers; I came to understand that I was being invited to work with God to promote healing. Because God has created human beings with intellects and hearts, God invites all of us to be co-healers and co-creators of our world. We can use our free wills to heal or harm. We can assist our brothers and sisters in their search for God, or, through our actions, we can make God's presence (and even existence) seem remote. The choice is ours. We can reject or accept Jesus' ministry as the template for our own ministry, a ministry available to both adults and children.

# Jesus and the Children

All three synoptic Gospels relay the story of Jesus and the children. Because it graphically describes Jesus' reaction to his disciples' turning away children, I quote the Marcan version here.

> People were bringing little children to him in order that he might touch them; and the disciples spoke sternly to them. But when Jesus saw this, he was indignant and said to them, "Let the little children come to me; do not stop them; for it is to such as these that the kingdom of God belongs. Truly I tell you, whoever does not receive the kingdom of God as a little child will never enter it." And he took them up in his arms, laid his hands on them, and blessed them (Mk 10:13–16).

In the previous chapter, Jesus had made another point about children.

> [Jesus asked his disciples,] "What were you arguing about on the way?" But they were silent, for on the way they had argued with one another who was the greatest. He (...) said to them, "Whoever wants to be first must be last of all and servant of all." Then he took a little child and put it among them; and taking it in his arms, he said to them, "Whoever welcomes one such child in my name welcomes me, and whoever welcomes me welcomes not me but the one who sent me" (Mk 9: 33–37).

Jesus understood that children *were* important because they are closer to the reign of God than adults. This was no sentimental reaction on Jesus' part, but a keen insight. Children have nothing that has not been given to them. That is true of adults as well, but we continue to fool ourselves into thinking that we are "self-made" men and women, or that we have "earned" what we have.

In the case of children, they *know* that they are dependent on adults for food, shelter, care, and affection. As such, they come with empty hands, confident that they will be filled by those who love them. In other words, they trust. Instead of turning children away, the disciples should have been learning from them. But, like all adults of all times, they firmly believed that adult ideas, speech, and projects were of primary importance. Thus, the disciples ignored the children or tried to remove them because they truly believed that Jesus had more important, *adult* projects on his mind. They really thought they were doing him a favor.

But they weren't, as Jesus pointed out (indignantly, at that). They weren't doing themselves a favor, either. In fact, they were missing the mark in terms of their understanding of the reign of God and true greatness in that reign.

Are we *that* different from those disciples of long ago? When we see families at church, do we ignore the children (or give them a cursory "hi") as we turn our attention to the parents? When we visit children in the hospital or at their homes, do we talk mostly with adults present rather than trying to connect with the children? When a child in our congregation dies, do we spend more time with their parents rather than their siblings who are old enough to understand? How do we support the children in the deceased child's classroom? Do we reassure ourselves that "kids don't understand these things; anyway, they'll get over it if we just ignore it"? If we are guilty of any of these reactions, we are imitating the disciples rather than Jesus. This book attempts to provide a different approach to ill children.

## How This Book Is Organized

In Part I of this book, chapters are devoted to each stage of development in childhood—cognitive, relational, and spiritual. A description of the pertinent stages from Jean Piaget, Erik Erikson, and James Fowler is presented for children under the best of circumstances. All three of these individuals developed their hypotheses by observing children in Western cultures. Hence, their work might not be generalizable to children of vastly different cultures. However, for the purposes of this book, most of the children to whom we minister will be those from Western cultures, and the hypothesized stages should apply well to them.

In the early years of the twentieth century, Piaget developed a hypothesis of how children learned, at various ages, by observing his own children. Later in the century, Erikson postulated how human beings develop relationships across the life span, although much of his work explored childhood. Finally, in the 1970s, Fowler explored how human beings develop faith by age. The work of these three individuals will form the theoretical basis of the chapters in Part I. A discussion of how illness affects children (and their families) at each stage is provided. Suggested pastoral approaches for children/teens and parents are offered.

In the second part of the book, particular circumstances

are described, and pastoral approaches to these (by age) are also provided.

Three comments are in order. First of all, children with certain physical challenges (such as blindness or deafness) are not treated in this book because they are *not* ill. This is also true of those with mental challenges such as mental retardation. Of course, when these children become acutely ill, require surgery, or are injured, they *then* fall into the categories treated by this book.

Second, when I speak of "ill," I am including recuperation after surgery as well. To keep verbiage to a minimum, I have not always spelled out the circumstances of children and teens who are recuperating from surgery, but they are certainly covered in this book.

Finally, I will be using the terms "child" and "teen" to refer to both genders. When using singular pronouns, I will alternate "he" and "she" or "him" and "her" in an attempt to be inclusive.

# A Word on Working With Health Professionals

My experience as a health professional has taught me that most health professionals feel the pain of their patients deeply, even if they don't express it openly. Most of us did not go into healthcare for the money, but instead out of a desire to help others. For most of us, that desire only deepens with time. We are frustrated and saddened when we cannot help or when someone refuses our overtures.

However, most of us were taught in professional schools that it is wrong to demonstrate any emotion with patients and their families. "Patients like to have strong, in-charge physicians," we were told. "They don't need or want someone to hold their hands. They don't need or want someone to cry with them." In medical school, I was taught this line of reasoning, and I accepted it. I also learned that if one of my patients died, it was because *I* didn't know enough, *I* hadn't studied hard enough. Whenever a child or teen died, I carried a huge burden, as a young physician. Was the death really all my fault because I had not studied hard enough or was ignorant?

I tell this story because it is important to realize that many health professionals have accepted this same line of reasoning and have suffered because of it. This notion forces one to pretend to know more than one really does so that one might never be accused of fault when a patient dies. It causes one to experience hours of soul-searching when a death occurs, even when it could not have possibly been prevented. When given the mantle of infallibility and omnipotence, disorientation results because one knows that he or she is neither all-knowing nor all-correct. Yet, the facade may be maintained.

Be sympathetic to the healthcare professionals with whom you come into contact. The brusque manner may be a cover for insecurities or remorse. Pray for health professionals, because we surely need all the prayers we can get. When a health professional wants to speak with you about the spiritual aspects of ill and dying children, listen. You may not agree with the person's theology (if he or she has one), but you are called to be present at that moment. And, who knows? Your presence might be the first chance that health professional ever had to be honest about their reactions to and questions about the misery all around them.

# PART ONE

# General Considerations

# CHAPTER 1

# What Parents and Siblings Experience When Children Are Ill

## Parental Reactions

Parents whose children are ill can be expected to experience any number of physical, emotional, and spiritual reactions. Although not every parent experiences *each* reaction, many experience most of them, although not necessarily in the order given.

### PHYSICAL

Having a child who is seriously ill or injured, chronically ill, or dying takes an enormous amount of energy from a parent. There is so much caregiving to provide, so much emotional support to give! Hence, parents feel chronically tired. They are trying to do too much for too many. Frequently, they do not attend to their own needs of diet, sleep, and exercise. Consequently, their own health suffers. They may be trying to work multiple jobs to secure adequate health insurance or income to pay for necessities. The fatigue and the stress may lead to loss of time from work, jeopardizing the income or healthcare which the family receives.

In addition to fatigue, many parents experience chronic pains or flare-ups of chronic conditions. Headaches, neck and shoulder pains or stiffness, backaches, and abdominal pain may be all due to stress as muscles tense or portions of the intestine go into spasm. With enough stress, some persons may experience conditions to which they have a susceptibility (for example, ulcers due to increased stomach acid production).

Persons with chronic conditions may experience worsening of symptoms. For example, skin conditions, allergies, or a spastic colon may worsen. More serious conditions such as ulcerative colitis, lupus, sarcoid, hypertension, and asthma may flare-up, sometimes leading to hospitalization. These flare-ups are mediated by the adverse effect of stress on the immune system. The immune system is a watchdog, protecting human beings from external germs and internal abnormalities (such as malignancies). A malfunctioning immune system makes it more likely that someone will be more susceptible to infections and internal malfunctions in the body. Alternatively, the immune system may go into overdrive and attack an individual's own body. For some parents, the stress is too much, and their immune systems do not adequately protect them, thus not only jeopardizing their own health but also the health of family members who depend on them.

Under the effect of stress, other parents become "accident-prone," whether due to inattention and distraction or a subconscious need to escape from their leadership role.

Some parents attempt to mask their stress and pain through the use of legal (for example, alcohol, prescription medications) or illegal drugs. Naturally, these drugs will also have their own physical effects.

## EMOTIONAL

The stress of having an ill child involves many aspects. In the case of a congenital malformation or infection, the parents (especially the mother) may feel enormous guilt that they caused the problem directly. For other conditions or injuries, parents may also feel guilty that they did not adequately protect their child when they should have done so. Loving parents suffer when they see their child undergo multiple medical procedures, especially when they realize that there is little that *they* can do to eliminate the discomfort or frank pain. Hence, a sense of helplessness results. This helplessness can lead to parental feelings of lowered self-esteem and worthlessness, and depression.

In two-parent families, the coping strategies of each parent may be so different that each of them feels that the other "doesn't understand"; this can lead to arguments and marital discord, which, in the end, harms a child who needs both parents. Because of fatigue, lowered self-esteem, and anger at each other (perhaps even blaming each other for the illness or injury), a loss of sexual intimacy can occur as one parent "saves" herself for the ill child rather than for the spouse. The other parent then feels left out and deserted. The primary caregiving parent can also feel deserted if she is left with the majority of child-care duties, especially if the spouse immerses himself in work or claims that he "has to work"; irritability and depression are common in both parents, but may be expressed very differently. These feelings, in turn, can lead to a dependence on substances (legal or illegal) or sexual experimentation with "someone who understands me." This is detrimental to the ill child or teen and further fractures the family.

Marriages also suffer when one parent accuses the other of "not caring" or "not being a good enough parent," or directly blames the other parent for the illness, condition, or injury with which the child suffers. Unfortunately, this is true not only in marriages but also of other relationships within the family, as family members assign blame to each other (for example, grandparents blaming parents, parents blaming their other children and vice versa, for the ill or injured child's condition).

## SPIRITUAL

The spiritual distress experienced by many parents cannot be overstated. Many parents question the existence of God or question the goodness of a God who permits small children to suffer. Parents wonder why *their* child in particular must suffer or whether God is punishing *them* for some real or imagined deed in the present or past. Many times, this offense is one which occurred long ago (such as an abortion or marital indiscretion); yet the parent feels that God has been keeping score and is "getting even" now.

Sometimes, the offense doesn't seem that awful to merit such terrible punishment from God. When parents believe that God is punishing them by the illness of their child or teen, they may reject the overtures of pastoral visitors, who are, after all, emissaries of the God whom they are questioning. They may be angry at God, and direct these feelings toward the pastoral visitors.

Other parents may be empty, unable to pray and unable to express their feelings about God. "Pray? You must be kidding," said one mother. "It's all I can do to take the next breath." They may feel as if they are in a desert or a wasteland. They may feel too disconsolate or too misunderstood to even hope for someone—especially a pastoral person—who can understand them.

## Siblings' Reactions

Depending on the ages of the siblings, their physical, emotional, and spiritual reactions may be very similar to that of their parents or very dissimilar. In general, the older the child, the more likely the reaction is to mirror that of adults. In addition, many children try to emulate a parent's reaction (or words), especially that of the parent of the same gender.

Even very young children feel a disruption of their lives when a sibling is ill, especially if a parent must be away from them to care for the ill sibling. There can be sleep or feeding disturbances in a young infant or periods of fussiness or crying. In toddlers and preschoolers, there may be a regression to behavior more typical of a younger age, for example, wanting a bottle, wanting to sleep in a crib, or urinary or bowel accidents. Verbal young children may also complain of aches and pains in an attempt to secure the parent's attention. After all, if the parent is interested in the sibling who is ill with various aches and pains, a sibling who is not ill may use illness to attract more attention. Preschool children might also be afraid that they caused a younger sibling's illness because they had been jealous of the child and maybe even wished harm to him.

In terms of death, young children simply do not understand that death is irreversible. Like cartoon characters which bounce back after being run over by trucks, preschoolers really believe that one who is dying *can* get better and one who has died *will* return.

In the elementary-school years, guilty feelings are heightened, because children of this age understand illness so much better than they did when they were younger. It is very common for siblings to fight with each other and to say mean things to each other, such as "I hate you. I wish you were dead" when they can't get their own way or when they want to annoy each other. When a sibling becomes ill, the child who made the comment might be consumed with guilt and feelings of self-loathing. "I didn't mean it when I said I wished she was dead," sobbed a six-year-old boy. "I didn't want her to get hit by a car." This type of "magical thinking" is common in the late preschool and early elementary-school years.

To deal with their guilt, such children might become weepy, distant, or argumentative and disobedient, depending on their own innate style and coping pattern. They might become mouthy at home, behavior problems in school, or irritants to those with whom they come into contact. Because the thought of having caused their sibling's illness or injury is so terrible, such children will do anything to draw attention away from that thought. In addition, acting out behaviors gets attention for them as well. True, it is not positive attention, but it *is* attention directed at them at a time when most of the attention is directed at their ill or injured sibling.

Physically, siblings may display chronic aches and pains, especially headaches and bellyaches. If they have a chronic medical condition, it may worsen. Some siblings take on the symptoms which their ill brother or sister have and become convinced that they have the same disease, or that they are going to die.

In terms of death, elementary-school children have learned that death is irreversible, and that the dead person can never return. Like many adults, they may be angry at the dead person for leaving them, believing that somehow the person had a choice. There is some evidence that a child's reaction to a sibling's death depends on the age and gender of both the dead child and the surviving child. Such children may also worry that they will be the next to die in the family, and that anxiety may play havoc with their peer relations, home life, and schoolwork.

As children become teens, their reactions are much more like those of adults, even stereotypically so. In other words, boys may believe that it is unmanly to cry or show emotion, especially if that is also a part of their ethnic heritage. Girls, on the other hand, may feel that a release of emotion is acceptable. In some cultures, this release may be so marked as to border on hysteria, yet, within that ethnic group, it is acceptable and even expected. Again, chronic aches and pains or worsening of preexisting conditions might surface, demonstrating the anxiety that the teen feels. Like elementary-school children, teens may worry that they are susceptible to the same disease that their sibling has.

Spiritually, children old enough to meaningfully converse often ask why God permits their sibling be so sick; if the sibling has died, they wonder why God took their sibling to heaven or why God didn't choose them for heaven. They might have questions about whether the dead sibling is being punished by being separated from the family. A few children will be very angry with God, while others will maintain that their sibling's death is not God's fault. Most children simply will not know what to believe. As such, they may either demonstrate *no* interest in church or a heightened interest in God. They may either scoff at the notion of a good God or cling to the notion that God loves them and has their best interests at heart. Generally speaking, the more cynical stances are taken by the older children and teens rather than the younger ones, and this is especially true if the older child or teen has a cynical adult role model to emulate.

# CHAPTER 2

# Preverbal Children: Infants and Toddlers

*Piaget Stage: Sensorimotor; Erikson Stage: Trust vs. Mistrust (Infancy), Autonomy vs. Shame and Guilt; Fowler Stage: Undifferentiated Faith*

## Stages in Health

Psychologist Jean Piaget was interested in how children learn. His first stage is called "sensorimotor." Simply stated, this means that infants and toddlers learn through their senses and through moving about and exploring objects. Infants and toddlers are also very alert to sights and sounds. The human face fascinates them, as do funny noises and (especially) the voices of those who are dear to them. Furthermore, infants go through a stage in which *everything* goes into their mouths. This is their way to explore their environment intimately. Once infants learn to move about independently (and become "toddlers," so named for their toddling gait), they are able to explore beyond their cribs, highchairs, and parents' arms.

Erik Erikson was interested in how human beings build relationships, not only with people but also with objects in their environment. In his first stage, Erikson noted that infants learn to trust the world (and those in it) by being treated well; conversely, they learn not to trust their world (and those in it) if their needs are ignored or ridiculed, or if they are harmed. By their second year of life, toddlers experience what Erikson called "autonomy vs. shame and guilt." Children in their second year of life are learning (and loving) to be independent in terms of movement, feeding, and (perhaps) toileting. When a child is not permitted to be independent, or when he fails in his attempts to be autonomous, shame and guilt can result. Obviously, with regard to both of these stages, some mistrust and shame and guilt occur because the world is not perfect and a child cannot always have her way. It is only when mistrust and shame/guilt define the child's existence that trouble in further stages of development can be expected.

James Fowler was interested in how faith develops. Leaning heavily on both Piaget and Erikson, Fowler developed a theory of faith development. He called the earliest stage a pre-stage (so named because we can't access children's thoughts directly in the first two years of life), and named it "undifferentiated faith." In agreement with Erikson, Fowler believed that children learn to have faith by experiencing faithfulness in the words and actions of those around them. For them to learn something about God, whom they can't see, they learn from human beings whom they do see. If a child is treated faithfully and receives positive messages about God, he learns to associate the word "God" with good thoughts, feelings, and actions. If a child is treated badly, receives negative messages about

God, especially messages that imply that God is on the side of adults against children, the word "God" will not be associated with goodness.

# Illness and Injury

When infants or toddlers are ill, their ability to learn in a sensorimotor fashion is limited. If they are hospitalized and have intravenous lines (IVs), they may be restrained and unable to touch and explore. Certainly, their mobility will be challenged. Even for less serious illnesses, they may be restricted in how much they are permitted to place in their mouths. Depending on their illness, their eyes may be covered, limiting their ability to use their vision to learn. A serious illness or injury will impact their ability to trust, since it seems that everyone coming to their room wants to poke or prod them, usually in a painful way. Even their parents cannot (or will not) save them from this treatment. In like manner, their faith in a peaceful existence may be challenged because of their experiences. Unfortunately, discomfort and pain are inherent parts of illness or injury.

It is, of course, difficult to watch any child suffer. Perhaps it is the hardest to observe small infants or toddlers because of the inability of adults to adequately explain things to them and to understand their wordless groans and cries. When faced with suffering children, most adults feel helpless. When one can engage in conversation with a child, one at least feels some competency in assisting him in coping with the situation. Not so with the youngest children. We can only watch their faces, hear their cries, and try to soothe little bodies racked by pain.

For some adults, the sights and sounds of young children in pain is unbearable, regardless of one's gender, medical sophistication, intelligence, or station in life. Although a potential minister to ill children and their families may be able to ask someone more suited to this type of ministry to make a visit, the minister should always keep in mind that the infant's parents do not get off so easily. *They* must be present for the benefit of their child; and when one parent is unable to cope in such circumstances, marital discord or dissolution might result.

Infants *feel* pain. In response to pain, they do what adults do. They grimace, flail their arms and legs, and cry lustily if they are able and have the strength to do so. When they are in pain, their heart rates and blood pressures rise, and their skin might change color to deep red or purple, especially when they are crying. This is true even of premature infants who have a breathing tube in place and whose cries cannot be heard. In addition, premature infants will be exquisitely sensitive to variations of temperature, noise, and lighting in a room. Because many of these infants are restrained to avoid their inadvertently pulling out needed IV lines or breathing tubes, they are limited in their movements—a far cry from the freedom of movement they experienced in utero.

Even with full-term infants and infants beyond the neonatal period, the expression of pain is obvious. Beyond the neonatal period, an infant might also be in distress because he cannot be held by the parent or is surrounded by persons unknown to the child. When this occurs after six months of age or so, a child can become frantic, especially if he has entered the stage of separation anxiety and stranger anxiety.

Separation anxiety is the fear of being separated from a parent (usually the mother) or significant adult. It is a normal stage of development, beginning between six to seven months of age and ending between twenty-four to thirty months of age. Children in this stage of development will cry and resist being held by someone else *even if* the parent or caregiver is in the same room.

Stranger anxiety is the fear of anyone who is not the parent (especially the mother) or significant adult. It, too, is entirely normal between the ages of six to seven months and twenty-four to thirty months. Again, even when her parent is holding her, a child in this stage of development will loudly object to the advances, however friendly, of someone unknown to her. Thus, added to the physical distress of a child in pain is the emotional distress of being separated from a parent and being surrounded by people whom she does not know. An infant's or toddler's emotional distress will contribute to parental emotional distress, because a loving parent doesn't want to be separated from her ill child and would prefer a situation in which there weren't so many strangers present.

As if all this was not bad enough—a relatively helpless infant or toddler who is suffering and who is separated from parents and surrounded by strangers—the situation in acute care settings may be much worse. Children suffer pain because of needed medical procedures. Although those committed to serving children's medical needs try to minimize any discomfort and do procedures as rapidly as possible, some procedures *do* hurt, even if only for a brief time. With an older child, one can explain that the "ouchy" after a needle stick will only last for a brief period. With an infant, one can say the same thing, but we simply don't know how much of our words are understood. Certainly, our tone of voice and manner *are* understood. Thus, a child is made even more miserable and frantic by the demeanor of a miserable and frantic parent, physician, or nurse. Unlike these adults, an infant is unable to adequately express his feelings.

In addition to procedures, ill children are also subjected to changes in their diets (for example, nothing by mouth or only clear liquids) and may experience hunger and frustration at not being fed in the manner to which they are accustomed. The infant may want to be held by a parent, but because of her precarious condition might need to remain in the crib, even restrained there. This is especially wrenching to parents who must stand by, unable to meet their child's needs. Feelings of guilt are common: "What kind of parent am I to not have been able to protect my baby from all of this?"

Although visitors can reassure parents that it isn't their fault, the fact remains that, in the parents' minds, it is their duty to protect their child from harm and suffering. Such guilt will be even more marked if the parent *was*, in fact, responsible for his child's situation. The suffering experienced by an infant exposed to cocaine in utero is wrenching for his addicted mother to witness. The child who was unrestrained in the car when it was hit and is now comatose breaks a parent's heart. The toddler who drank the lye that was under the sink and is now on a life-support system evokes in a caring parent a deep self-recrimination. The child who was abused by a relative and is now lying bleeding in the emergency room fills a parent with rage both at the perpetrator and himself for not having been there to prevent it.

We should not be too quick to judge parents who "should have known better," or "should have been more careful." Have we never made mistakes with children in our care? Have we never been careless or out of control? Have we never been too tired to notice or too ill to think properly? The truth is that we've *all* been there at some point in our lives. Jesus said, "Let the one who is without sin cast the first stone." Who among us is without sin and is eligible for the privilege of casting that first stone?

# Pastoral Approaches to Infants and Toddlers and Their Families

1. When you enter the room, do so quietly. Although smiling at an infant or toddler is appropriate, too much closeness too soon may frighten him. Be friendly but not overbearing. Do not stare at him.
2. Although you can ask a parent how her infant or toddler is doing, don't pry. Allow her to tell you as much as she wants. Also, don't offer advice because you may not know the person or situation well enough to do so.
3. Always ask a parent's permission to pray for an infant or small child in the hospital room. You can pray silently or aloud for the child, perhaps resting your hand on the top of her head. Unless you are sure that your hands are clean, avoid touching an infant's or toddler's hands or face.
4. If an infant or child is fearful of a visitor's approach, then by all means keep a distance and pray from afar. Similarly, no attempts to hold an infant or toddler or to touch him should be made against his will.

5. Praying aloud should include simple prayers which are familiar to the child you are visiting; the Lord's Prayer may be very appropriate here. The infant's or toddler's parent can also suggest prayers which are routinely said at home.

6. Singing simple songs is also a good way to pray, since most infants and toddlers are fascinated by singing. If they are familiar with a song, hearing it will calm them.

7. Ministry to a suffering infant or toddler includes ministry to the suffering parent also. Although we are not sure how much a young infant or toddler can understand, we do know that parents can be positively or negatively affected by what visitors (however well-meaning) say. Well-intentioned but ill-conceived statements may not only hurt a parent emotionally but also spiritually, especially if statements about God's judgment or will are included. Avoid offering unsolicited advice. If your advice is solicited, first find out how the parent feels about the issue at hand. Above all, do not take sides when there are disagreements between the parents or between the parents and other relatives.

8. Parents should be asked if *they* want the visitor to pray with them (silently or aloud). In addition, parents should be given the option of leading the prayer themselves. Although many parents decline this invitation, others appreciate it and embrace it. Unless the visitor knows a parent well, the parent should *always* be asked her preference in these matters. If a parent refuses prayer by the visitor at the time of the visit, respect these wishes. You can always pray for the child and parent when you leave the room. At such a vulnerable time, no attempt should be made to force a parent to seek God.

9. Always ask if there is anything that you or the congregation can do for the family. In particular, ask if it is OK to visit again. Then, abide by the wishes of those closest to the infant. If you promise to visit again, do so.

# CHAPTER 3

# Preschoolers

*Piaget Stage: Preoperational; Erikson Stage: Initiative vs. Guilt; Fowler Stage: Intuitive-Projective*

## Stages in Health

According to Piaget, in the preschool years, children learn in a "preoperational" manner. Simply stated, that means that their thought processes are non-logical. They have not yet learned such formal operations of listing, counting, categorizing, reasoning. Hence, their ideas on things are rather fanciful! They have no concept of time. They are highly creative, open to new ideas, and excited by life.

During this stage, according to Erikson, children are learning to take initiative—taking care of themselves to a degree and performing simple chores. If their attempts are met with success, they will learn to trust their initiative and their abilities; if their attempts are usually unsuccessful or met with ridicule or anger by significant adults in their lives, they will learn not to try at all. In such cases, their creativity, openness, and enthusiasm are stifled.

Fowler's faith stage closely mirrors Piaget's stage in the preschool years. Fowler believed that children were intuitive, that is, had insights about things and people which were not formally taught to them. Intuition goes hand-in-hand with creativity and openness. But, preschoolers also project; that is, they make judgments about people and things based on their experiences with similar people and things in their past. In terms of preschoolers' ideas about God, they have many insights that we adults don't have. These ideas are not necessarily wrong, just different from those of adults. They are open to learning more about God and enthusiastic about what God has done.

On the other side of this stage, preschoolers project onto God the attributes that they have seen in significant adults around them. If these attributes are positive (kindness, goodness, generosity, forgiveness), children will also project these to God. If the attributes experienced are negative (punishing, judging, holding grudges, ridiculing), a child may well project these attributes onto God. This is especially true if the child routinely hears adults speak carelessly or disparagingly about God.

## Illness and Injury

When preschoolers are seriously ill, they are usually not encouraged to take initiative because of their condition. Hence, many children regress to younger ways of behaving. This is to be expected, especially in light of the fact that parents overtly (or covertly) encourage these behaviors through the manner in which they treat ill children. Preschoolers may have very imaginative explanations for why they are ill, needed an operation, or were injured. "Late at night, the monster under my bed grabbed my tummy. It hurt until I went to the doctor who cut me," said a four-year-old with appendicitis. "I got sick when I fell asleep in the car," said a three-year-old with dehydration due to an intestinal virus.

They also can project: "My daddy got sick after he painted my room, and I got sick after I colored in my coloring book." Because her father had been painting before he became ill, she reasons that her own illness is due to the act of coloring. In terms of God's role in their illness, children of this age can attribute illness to a God who punishes them for doing wrong: "I got sick because I laughed at my baby brother when he was sick last week," moaned a four-year-old boy. Never mind that the baby's illness and the big brother's illness are not the same. It's a bit of "an eye for an eye, a tooth for a tooth." (Come to think of it, this belief is shared by many adults.)

Unlike the younger age group, children of this age can (and do) communicate verbally. This ability obviously improves with age, so that the average four-year-old is much better able to describe his feelings than the average two-year-old. That does not mean, however, that the two-year-old does not have the very same feelings as the older child or does not need to communicate these feelings in some way.

Clearly children of this age feel pain and usually express their distress by crying, screaming, or thrashing. If preschoolers have learned to swear because of the example given to them by household members, they may say bad words in response to pain. The wise pastoral visitor is not shocked by this, and does not use the visit to sermonize about the ill child's language or the parents' child-rearing skills.

More reserved children or those socialized by stoical parents may quietly whimper or, at the extreme, remain silent. Preschoolers may react to physical pain or emotional pain (for example, the threat of separation from the parent) with anger and may make less than polite comments, such as "I hate you," "You're stupid," "I wish you were dead," and "Go away." Such statements should not be judged too harshly. Although it *is* inappropriate for a child to verbally abuse another person, the context in which the verbal abuse is taking place must be considered. In addition, if a child has heard parents or other significant adults use profanity when they are upset, she may do likewise, regarding it as a "grown-up" thing to do. Although verbal abuse might be understandable (for example, every time the nurse comes into the room, the child receives an injection, and so he associates the nurse with pain), it is never to be treated lightly or considered to be humorous.

Physical abuse must be firmly and consistently discouraged. Biting, spitting, hitting, or throwing objects in order to hurt someone is *never* acceptable, no matter how much a child is hurting. Preschoolers *do* have poor impulse control, and that is true even when they are perfectly healthy. Many preschoolers (as well as some toddlers) have tantrums whenever they do not get their way. Hence, discharge of built-up negative psychic energy must be permitted because they are common, especially in such trying circumstances as illness and injury. Adults are encouraged to teach a child how to find other (safer) ways of discharging that energy, such as hitting a pillow, drawing furiously, making an audiotape in which one says what's on one's mind, and so on.

Separation issues still loom large, and it is inappropriate for parents, other relatives, or medical staff to urge a child to be a "big boy" or "big girl." The fact of the matter is that preschoolers are babes no matter how rapidly adults want them to grow up. Thus, it is *completely* appropriate for a four-year-old to scream, cry, or reach for a parent when wheeled out of her hospital room by a stranger who will not permit that parent to accompany her. It is *completely* appropriate for a three-year-old undergoing a lumbar puncture (spinal tap) to resist being held down and to call loudly for his mother when she is asked to step out of the room for the procedure.

At times such as these, parents need all the support they can receive. They feel guilty enough that their child is ill or injured and must endure more pain in order to get well. Now they are faced with their own sense of inadequacy that they cannot be present to support their child emotionally in time of need. Many parents respond to this inadequacy by crying themselves; others become hostile and talk aggressively ("Don't worry, son. If they hurt you, daddy will beat them up.").

Even pastoral visitors can be the brunt of these comments ("You don't have to talk to the mean, old pastor if you don't want to, honey" a mother said to her frightened three-year-old before her surgery. Explained the mother to the pastor, "Your black outfit scares her.").

# Pastoral Approaches

1. First of all, approach a child gently. Say hello and identify yourself. Smile and use a soft tone of voice. If the child's eyes meet yours, play with him a bit, either with a toy or an activity, like hide-and-seek (with the visitor hiding behind a door and then reappearing). If the child will not permit his eyes to meet yours, don't stare at him. Instead, be present silently and give the child space to be himself. Wise ministers to families with ill children know not to take negative comments made by a child (or his stony silence) personally.

2. Introduce yourself to the parent or other adults in the room. Do not talk to an adult as if the child is not present; that is rude. For example, to ask a parent, "How is Johnny?" when Johnny has just refused to speak sends a message that Johnny's opinion is not important. Instead, it is perfectly acceptable to ask the parent, "How do *you* think Johnny is doing?" because *that* is a question that Johnny himself cannot answer.

3. When a child does wish to talk, what can one possibly say? Let the child lead. Many times, she will ask questions. Children of this age normally have a number of questions, and they usually ask them easily. When something happens that preschoolers don't understand, they will repeatedly ask, "Why?" If this happens in good times, it will certainly happen in the not-so-good times if the child thinks that her parents will accept and answer questions. Sometimes, children understand that their parents do not want questions, or that they are too upset to be "bothered." These children will not ask

their questions, at least not of their parents, although they might ask them of others. Questions about the child's condition ("What's wrong with me?"), activity ("Can I eat ice cream?"), procedures ("Am I going to get a needle?"), and presence of parents ("Can my mommy stay with me?") are common.

4. Children who have been churched or, at least, have heard about God frequently ask more spiritual questions as well ("Why does God let me be sick?" "Why doesn't God make me better?" "Why doesn't God make my mommy and daddy stop crying?"). These questions can *never* be passed off as the innocent musings of children too young to understand anything of substance. If we cannot demonstrate God's presence and love in the midst of illness and trial to those who are hurting, we will never be able to demonstrate it in better times. This is true not only of adults but also (and especially) of children, even the youngest ones.

5. Children who are hurting want to know that God is for them, that God is not on the side of hurt or illness. Because young children understand things differently than adults do, they may think that they are ill because they were "bad." Some children, for example, are denied dessert when they have misbehaved. Thus, when a young child is not permitted to eat normally in the hospital, he may think that he has been bad to merit this "punishment." Similarly, many children are denied the opportunity to go out and play when they have misbehaved. When such children are not permitted to leave their hospital rooms, is it any wonder that they interpret it as punishment?

6. The questions asked by children must be answered in a

way that honors their developmental level *and* seeks to be as honest as possible under the circumstances. For example, if a child asks, "Was I hit by the car because I was bad?" a response might be, "No, your leg is broken not because you were bad. Your leg is broken because a car hit you when you were in the street. Even though your mom told you not to go into the street, the car didn't hit you just because you didn't listen to her." If a child says, "God won't let me eat now because I threw my green beans into the garbage can," a response might be, "God doesn't work that way. You can't eat because you are sick, not because God is mad at you for throwing food away. Even though it isn't a good thing to throw food away, that is not the reason you can't eat now."

7. Some children are worried that God won't know where they are: "Does God know I'm in the hospital?" asked a worried five-year-old. When reassured that God did, the child sighed, "But I can't see him" (making reference to the absence of the cross which hangs in his bedroom at home). In such a case, it would be good to bring the cross to the child's room not only so that he could have a familiar possession with him but also that he could experience God with him.

8. In my experience, children of this age rarely ask if they are going to die. This is because they do not understand death as an irreversible event. When young children are very ill, they are more worried about being separated from parents and siblings, whether they will hurt, and who will take care of their family or pets while they're away. Hence, these questions can be answered simply and honestly. For example, "The doctors and

nurses will try to make it so that you won't hurt" or "When you're not at home, your brother will take care of your rabbit."

9. In the case of a dying preschooler, older siblings must receive consolation in addition to their parents. Siblings old enough to understand death wonder why their younger sibling is being punished with illness. Or they might wonder why the younger child was selected to "go to God" rather than them ("Aren't I good enough?" asked a seven-year-old). Adults must watch their language carefully and avoid saying such things as "Molly is going on a long trip," "Molly is going to sleep for a long time," or "God needs another little angel in heaven, and God has chosen Molly." Any of these comments can lead an older child to wonder "Why can't I go on a long trip?" "Why does Molly need to sleep for a long time?" "Am I ever going to sleep and not wake up?" or "Why does God need Molly to be an angel? Can't God just make another angel?"

10. When praying with preschoolers, simple prayers are the best, especially if the child knows them already. Do not immediately ask a child if he wants to pray upon entering his room. Socialize a bit first. If a child says that he doesn't want to pray, ask if he minds if *you* pray aloud. If the answer is "no," do so. If the child indicates that he doesn't want you to pray aloud, pray silently. If the parent tries to contradict the child's wishes, take the child's side. After all, he is the ill one.

11. Ministry to a suffering preschooler includes ministry to the suffering parent, remembering that the parent can be positively or negatively affected by what visitors say. Well-intentioned but ill-conceived statements

can not only hurt a parent emotionally but also spiritually, especially if statements about God are included.
It is important for the pastoral visitor to help mothers
and fathers see what good parents they have been. This
is best done through quiet conversation and encouragement, in effect, bringing a distressed person to a
calmer level. Above all, avoid giving unsolicited advice.
If your opinion is sought on a particular matter, first
listen to the parent's perceptions about it before ren-
dering your own opinion (if at all). Do not take sides if
there are disagreements between the parents or between
the parents and other relatives.

12. There is no set formula on how to minister. Some parents respond well to quiet conversation; others do better by being held; still others prefer to simply have a
supportive person silently in the room with them. Treat
each situation as a unique event and each family as
unique individuals.

13. As with infants and toddlers, issues of why this illness
or this disease happened to this child will arise. It is
always best not to suggest rational human answers to
issues that are nonrational. For example, who can say
why one sibling has cancer while the others are completely well? Who can say why one child is paralyzed
after a motor vehicle accident while the sibling, in the
same section of the car, walked away with minor injuries? The most important thing is to be present in the
midst of the family's pain. Answers to such questions
are not really expected, but the need to ask such questions—without fear of rejection—is paramount. No
matter how much theological training a pastoral visitor has received, hospital or hospice rooms may not be

the places to demonstrate it. Hospitals, hospices, and homes are places to manifest God's loving care to those who need evidence of this the most.

14. Parents should be asked if *they* want the visitor to pray with them (silently or aloud); if they decline, respect that. In addition, parents should be given the option of leading the prayer themselves. Although many parents decline this invitation to lead prayer, others appreciate it and embrace it. Unless the visitor knows a parent well, the parent should *always* be asked her preference in these matters.

15. Before leaving, ask the parent if there is anything that you or your congregation can do for her. Don't assume that you know what any given parent needs; always ask. Some of what is needed might be practical (for example, taking his carpooling turn), while other needed gifts might be more emotional in nature (for example, being able to call you when she just wants to talk). Certainly, all parents can benefit from prayers, but ask if they want their names published or spoken publicly at worship services. Some parents, especially in difficult times, need their privacy. Respect that. Also remember to ask if the other parent or other children in the family need anything. Finally, ask if you may visit again. And remember, abide by the answers that you are given; if you promise to do something or have someone else do something, keep that promise to the best of your ability. At such a vulnerable time as a child's illness, a failure to follow up on a promise (even though it may have been due to simple forgetting) may be perceived by a parent as rejection or lack of concern.

# CHAPTER 4

# School-Age Children

*Piaget Stage: Concrete Operations; Erikson Stage: Industry vs. Inferiority; Fowler Stage: Mythic-Literal*

## Stages in Health

According to Piaget, children of this age learn in a literal fashion and are very concrete. They are socialized in school to take advantage of this characteristic. They learn such concrete facts as numbers and the alphabet when they are younger and historical dates and manipulation of numbers in mathematics when they are older. They enjoy mastering subjects and projects. They like to know how things work and how broken things get repaired. They like to learn new facts and seem to be continuously awed by nature and the world. Emotionally, they become dedicated to their friends and classmates, widening their social circle beyond that of their immediate family. They want to be in charge of certain things for themselves and demonstrate this competency to their friends.

In terms of a child's relationship to others and to the world, Erik Erikson noted that this seemed to be an age of industry (that is, working hard, especially in school). If the hard work does not pay off, however, a sense of inferiority sets in. After all, no matter how hard some children work, they will *never* be the best speller or mathematician in their class. No matter how hard some children try, they will *never* be the best at sports or dancing. No matter how much certain children try, they will *not* be able to make friends easily. Friends are important at this age because they verify a child's beliefs about himself. True, parents and siblings can do that, but they're family. When someone outside one's family is a true friend, one has achieved a real friendship.

In classifying their stage of faith, James Fowler noted Piaget's emphasis on elementary-school children's concreteness. In terms of their faith development, Fowler called them "mythic-literal": literal in the sense that they are *very* concrete (for which they are rewarded in school), and mythic in the sense that they appreciate stories that are larger than life. This is the age at which children love to read or hear stories about superheroes and superheroines, and this love extends to stories from Scripture as well. Children love to hear stories that evoke a "Wow!" from them, whether it is Jesus raising Lazarus or Moses crossing the Red Sea. At the same time, they want to hear those stories verbatim. If the story says that Jesus fed 5,000, it wasn't 4,999 or 5,001! If Scripture says a patriarch was 120 years old, it is useless to tell children of this age that the number may be symbolic instead of actual. This is a great age to capitalize on child's love of Scripture stories and to present as many as one can in a lively way.

# Illness and Injury

In times of illness or injury, however, the sense of competency possessed by most elementary-school children can take a serious blow, especially if they cannot feed themselves, or if they need assistance to go to the bathroom. They feel like "babies" and, for the most part, dislike the dependence that illness brings, even though they may revert to behaviors that they used at younger ages such as whining.

Furthermore, they may be frustrated or angered by restrictions placed on their activities or diet, especially if they are mentally aware of how limited this illness or injury has made them. Although they might feel ill, they still want to be the ones who call the shots.

They also worry that they might miss too much school and have to be "left behind." This is especially troubling because, through no fault of their own, they might have to repeat a grade and make all new friends, because their friends won't want to be with a "dummy," which in their minds is the name for anyone left behind. Thus, a hospital or home tutor is important in permitting an ill or injured child to remain current with her schoolwork.

Elementary-school children feel cheated when they do not improve after they have been "good," that is, doing everything that the doctor said that they needed to do in order to get better. Because of their literal, concrete sense, if the doctor says Johnny can go home tomorrow morning if he eats his supper tonight, Johnny expects to do just that, even if Johnny was up all night with a high fever and vomiting. Johnny will protest, "But you promised!" while the doctor will say, "But, you got sick last night." Even though Johnny knows this to be true, his sense of fairness has been violated because he *did* eat his supper. He kept his part of the deal. The doctor is the one who went back on her word, not Johnny.

Because of their keen verbal skills, children of this age articulate what they are feeling. Their comments might be full of anger and even profanity. They can be rude to anyone who comes into their rooms to visit and to hospital personnel who must do procedures with them. Even (or especially) their parents evoke their ire, probably because parents are safe. After all, what will happen to them if they explode at a nurse or doctor? Will they get a needle or be placed in isolation? Even though needles and isolation are not used as means of punishment when children are ill or injured, these very literal children understand only too well that when they are "bad" they are sent to their room, alone, or they go without food, leading to hunger pain. Doing a bit of projecting, they see any limitation of their diet, activity, or visitors as punishment because that is their lived experience. Doctors and nurses can't strike them, but they can give needles. Thus, it is *always* wrong for an adult to say to a child, "If you don't do what I say, I'm going to ask the doctor to give you a needle."

Sometimes, elementary-school children act their age (or older); at other times, they act much younger. At times, ill or injured elementary-school children want their parents and siblings to leave; at other times, they don't want to be alone. At times, they are weepy; at other times, they are giggly or they demonstrate incredible bravado. At times, they feel grownup; at other times, they feel like babies (and want to be treated accordingly). They may be so angry that they throw things; they might be so docile that they initiate and welcome hugs with everyone.

In keeping with their developmental stage, they ask many questions, expecting concrete, literal answers. "Why do you need to draw my blood?" "To run some tests." "What tests?" "Tests for your kidneys." "Why?" On and on. In the end, no answer completely satisfies them because, most of all, they want to be at home and "normal" again.

Many of these reactions described depend, of course, on how ill the child feels and how his coping strategies have worked in the past. Children who feel very ill may well lash out; children who are mildly ill may be more tolerant. On the other hand, some children who feel very ill may be far more tolerant than those who are mildly ill. It is not only a function of a child's innate temperament but also of the behaviors modeled by significant adults in his family or neighborhood.

Spiritually, these children ask concrete questions of God and anyone who claims to know something about God. "Why did God pick me to be sick of all the kids in my class?" cried an eight-year-old girl with leukemia. "Why is it that my roommate got to go home after his operation and I'm still here after mine? Doesn't God want me to be better?" asked a frustrated seven-year-old boy. "If the people at church pray for me, will I get better sooner?" asked a nine-year-old boy. Alternatively, a ten-year-old girl asked, "If all those people at church have been praying so hard for me—like they say they have—then why aren't I better? Am I still sick because I was bad?"

This last question is a particularly hard one because children are frequently warned by well-meaning parents with such tried-and-true comments as "If you don't wear your coat buttoned up, you're going to get a cold!" Illness seems like the natural consequence of disobeying one's parents. And so, when one is seriously ill, the elementary-school child thinks that she must have done something very, very wrong to deserve such a fate. Often, children of this age will drive themselves crazy trying to figure out just what God is angry about.

Furthermore, if the doctors have to do painful procedures (causing more pain), the child will conclude that he must have been really evil. Such thoughts do not bring comfort to a child's mind or heart, especially if he has also been taught to regard God as the one who doles out punishment for the things we have all done wrong. In such a child's mind, God will not seem to be his ally, and he might become afraid of God or angry at God for "giving" him the illness or letting it happen.

When elementary-school children are dying, frequently they know even if their parents or medical staff have not told them. "I think I'm dying, but don't tell my mother," whispered one nine-year-old child with cancer, "because she doesn't know yet, and I don't want to worry her." "Jesus is coming for me tonight," said a boy with cystic fibrosis, "but my mom and dad aren't ready, and they're too scared." Other children face their impending death with real anger and a sense that they are being cheated. "It's so sad," said an eight-year-old girl dying of AIDS, "because I'll never grow up to be a lady and a teacher. I would have been a really good one."

# Pastoral Approaches

1. When entering an elementary-school child's room, smile at the parent, if present, but acknowledge the child *first*. Greet the child, greet the child, greet the child! Upon entering the room, greet him, identify yourself, and ask how he is. If the child turns away, respect that and don't force conversation. If his TV is on, you could ask, "Do you mind if I watch your TV for a few minutes?" But if he responds, "Go away," then leave. You can always pray silently for him after you go. If the child shrugs his shoulders or says, "Yeah, you can watch my TV," then stay, but don't chatter on. Watch the TV. Never say to a child, "Well, if you won't talk to me, then I'll just talk to your mom (or dad)." Such a comment reenforces, in the child's mind, that you only came to talk to the "important" people (that is, the adults) anyway. The child may not want to talk because he is tired or in pain. We would honor an adult's wishes who was tired or in pain. The situation is no different for children.

2. Never talk to an adult in the room as if the child is not present. When Petra ignores you, resist the temptation to say to the parent, "How is she doing?" If Petra wanted to tell you, she would have said so herself. Instead, ask the parent, "How do *you* think Petra is doing?" That is a question that the parent can rightly answer and one that Petra cannot.

3. When (and if) the child wants to talk, ask what she would like to talk about. Don't assume you know her preferred topics of conversation. Safe topics are usually

hobbies and interests, recently read books, recently seen movies, favorite TV shows, and so on. In other words, the conversation is about the *child's* interests.

4. Usually conversation about the child's family or school is safe, but not always, so be as sensitive as you can possibly be. For example, if there are marital problems, and the parents are about to split, don't talk about the family. If you know that the child desperately wants to be in school, don't say something like, "Do you know what you missed in school this week? A clown visited your class! Everyone knew you would have loved to have been there." Such a comment will make him feel even more left out. It would be better to say, "Your class-mates really miss you and hope you get better soon so you can be with them. Things aren't the same without you." In other words, let the child ask you what has happened in the last week, and don't volunteer infor-mation that could sadden or anger him.

5. When comfortable, children of this age will readily ex-press themselves, sometimes with less than polite lan-guage. Although illness does not excuse poor manners, adults need to make allowances for children who are in pain or suffering emotionally and need to be not as easily offended as they might be with a healthy child who makes similar comments. Try not to take rude lan-guage personally. Children are immature, and they vary in their abilities to handle stress (as do adults). Parents can gently use these stressful situations to teach their children better methods of handling frustration and pain, but it is not the pastoral visitor's place to do so.

6. Under no circumstances should the intentional physi-cal harming of another person be permitted. If the child

you are visiting is obviously angry and throwing objects, leave. She will calm down eventually, but unless you know this child well, *you* will probably not be the agent of promoting this state of calm.

7. If the child begins to cry, permit him to do so and do not try to stop it because of *your* discomfort. Crying is a normal reaction to frustration, fear, or pain—all of which may be operant in the life of an ill child. When a child is crying, ask if he would like a tissue or if he would like you to leave. Abide by the response that you receive. Above all, do not attempt to minimize the tears by making jokes or distracting the child unless you know him well enough to know that such an approach is helpful. Minimizing pain only trivializes it.

8. Children of this age are frequently very cognizant of the fact that they are terminally ill or actively dying. This may make them frightened or angry initially, but, with enough time, most children come to accept their situations. Many children will not talk about dying because they are afraid their parents or visitors don't know what's going on. In spite of this, they have many questions. If such questions are posed to you, answer as honestly and gently as you can. For example, if a child asks you if she can eat chocolate in heaven, say something like, "I don't know for sure because I've never been there, but I hope so! What do you think?" This is honest (*you* have never been to heaven so you don't know what occurs there), sensitive (if a child brings up chocolate, she must be hoping that chocolate is in heaven), and friendly (like the child, you, too, hope that there is chocolate in heaven, that pets are in heaven, and so on).

9. Keep in mind that a child may be angry at God because of his illness. This is not always true, but it occurs often enough to make mention of it here. Many children have been taught by their parents that God rewards goodness and punishes evil. When a child is seriously ill or injured, she may wonder what she did that was so wrong to deserve her condition. A pastoral visitor must be ready to hear some anger directed toward God without reprimanding the child or trying to teach the child a lesson. Because God has given us all free will, God permits us to respond to divine overtures freely. If that is true of adults, it is also true of children. If a child asks you a question about God, be as honest as you can be, remembering the child's developmental level and her current circumstances. Remember, in times of serious illness or injury—especially if there is pain—no human being is at their best.

10. Reassure the child of God's love. Reassure the child that God is present, even in the hospital or sickroom. If at all possible, let the child have some personal possession that reminds her of God and brings her comfort. Ask about favorite Bible stories and why they are the child's favorite. Offer to read those stories to her, or to obtain a book of these stories for her.

11. Ask the child if he would like to pray with you. Do not force this prayer; after all, God doesn't force adults to pray! You can always pray alone for this child and for his family. If the child declines prayer, don't push it. Don't ask if he minds if you pray, *if his response won't make any difference*. In other words, if you are going to pray anyway, don't ask the child if it's okay for you to do so.

12. If the child agrees to prayer, ask her if she would like to lead the prayer. Many elementary-school children prefer to lead prayers, so don't assume that you should lead them. Also, ask the child which prayers she would prefer.

13. If the parent interrupts or tries to answer for a child who is alert, gently indicate that you really want to hear what the child has to say.

14. Ministry to a suffering child includes ministry to the suffering parent, remembering that the parent can be positively or negatively affected by what visitors say. Well-intentioned but ill-conceived statements can not only hurt a parent emotionally but also spiritually, especially if statements about God's judgment or will are included. It is important for the pastoral visitor to help mothers and fathers see what good parents they have been. This is best done through quiet conversation and encouragement, in effect, bringing a distraught parent to a calmer, more rational level. Avoid giving unsolicited advice. If your opinion is solicited, always inquire about parental opinions before giving your own. Above all, do not take sides if there are disagreements between the parents, between the parents and other relatives, or between the child and her parents or other relatives.

15. There is no set formula on how to minister. Some parents respond well to quiet conversation; others do better by being held; still others prefer to simply have a supportive person silently in the room with them. Treat each situation as a unique event and each family as unique individuals.

16. As with younger children, issues of why this illness or this disease happened to this child will arise. It is al-

ways best not to suggest rational human answers to issues that are non-rational. For example, who can say why one sibling has AIDS while another is completely well? Who can say why one child is in a coma after a motor vehicle accident while the sibling, in the same section of the car, walked away with minor injuries? The important thing is to be present in the midst of the family's pain. Answers to such questions are not really expected, but the need to ask such questions without fear of rejection is paramount.

17. Parents should be asked if *they* want the visitor to pray with them (silently or aloud)—separately from the child, if necessary; if they decline, respect that. In addition, parents should be given the option of leading the prayer themselves. Although many parents decline this invitation to lead prayer, others appreciate it and embrace it. Unless the visitor knows a parent well, the parent should *always* be asked her preference in these matters.

18. Before leaving, ask the parent if there is anything that you or your congregation can do for her. Don't assume that you know what any given parent needs; always ask. Some of what is needed might be practical (for example, taking his carpooling turn), while other needed gifts might be more emotional in nature (for example, being able to call you when she just wants to talk). Certainly, all parents can benefit from prayers, but ask if they want their names published or spoken publicly at worship services. Some parents, especially in difficult times, need their privacy. Respect that. Also remember to ask if the other parent or other children in the family need anything. And, finally, ask both parent and

child if it is okay for you to visit again—and take the child's response as seriously as you take the parent's. Failure to keep a promise—especially with regard to making a return visit—may be interpreted as rejection or lack of concern, not only on the part of the pastoral visitor but also on the part of God, whose representative you are.

# CHAPTER 5

# Preteens and the Early Teenagers

*Piaget Stage: Formal Operations; Erikson Stage: Identity vs. Role Diffusion; Fowler Stage: Synthetic-Conventional*

## Stages in Health

Piaget understood that, at this age, young people are stretching their limits. No longer children, they are coming into contact with persons quite different from their family members, and they are encountering novel situations. These situations occur because young people have more independence and more mobility than they did when they were younger. Hence, these experiences open up new worlds for them. They can imagine themselves being in novel situations, can imagine what it would be like to be someone other than themselves, and can place themselves in others' situations. They are beginning to seriously dream about what they want to do when they become adults. Reasoning powers are more keen than they have been previously, and this capacity is used to good advantage to prepare them for adulthood. Piaget called these processes "formal operations."

In the midst of the novel experiences, young adolescents are trying to forge their own identities, separate from those of their parents. Erikson emphasized that young persons might have to "try on" a variety of roles in order to discern who they really are. From the young adolescent's perspective, it makes perfect sense to sample as many experiences (or as many friends) as possible; from the adult perspective, the behaviors of young adolescents seem "scattered."

This plays into a young adolescent's faith experience as well. Fowler reasoned that persons of this age had just recently been children who had been quite literal in their approach to their faith. Some of that still is operant, and encourages young adolescents to be "conventional," that is, to embrace at least part of what they have experienced before. Yet, all the novel experiences show them that other people, people who seem, at least on the surface, to be "good," don't necessarily believe as they do. For example, a young adolescent who has been taught that "good" people always attend church services on Sundays comes into contact with seemingly "good" people who never attend church services. Or, as another example, it becomes clear to the young adolescent that not all persons of the same denomination hold the same beliefs. So, which is right—what parents have taught them or what they see in others? It is no wonder that this is so disconcerting; after all, just a few short years before, these same young people were *so* sure, so literal. Now, that surety has evaporated.

This is the age in which children are beginning to question their faith or the practices of their faith. They may start to seriously grumble about going to church. They may become fascinated with non-Christian practices. In other words, they are beginning to "synthesize" a belief system that may have components from a number of traditions.

# Illness and Injury

Being physically and emotionally ill is very draining for anyone, especially those who are at the beginning of active social lives away from their families. In the developmental stage of separating from parents, preteens and young teens seek independence and come to rely more on the opinions and support of peers. When a young person is ill, she is by necessity prevented from spending as much time as she would like with peers. In addition, she may be physically dependent on her parents, which is very difficult at this age, especially if the parent must help the young teen feed or toilet herself.

Young people of this age want to fit in and be like everyone else. Illness or injury ensures a situation in which a preteen or young teen will look different or need to be treated differently than the "gang." He may not be able to eat with his friends because of dietary restrictions or the need to take medications at certain times on an empty stomach. She is embarrassed by the fact that she has lost her hair, must wear a wig, or needs special equipment to get around. Most of these ill young people are sensitive to others' glances and giggles, even when they are not directed at them. Although these young teens need their parents' support and reassurance, they also *need* approval of their peers.

Preteens and young teens are known for having a great deal of energy, and illness saps that energy. This can be enormously depressing because young adolescents know how they used to be and what they are now missing socially. They wonder if they will ever be well enough again to engage in sports, dance, date, or party. They try to push themselves too hard and too fast; when they fail, they become easily frustrated or angry at themselves and those closest to them. Those closest to them—their parents, siblings, or best friends—are "safe" in the sense that there is less likelihood of frank rejection by them. Ill adolescents may have periods of intense hostility to those closest to them—angry one minute and weeping the next.

In addition, these students miss the social and academic environment of school and the regular routine of the school day. They worry that they will miss too much school and may fail, thus being left behind from their same-age peers. Since only "dummies" fail, they too must be dumb. Who will then be their friends—the same-age peer group who are now a year ahead or the younger group with whom the ill adolescent must now attend classes? Failing because of illness is still *failing*; it is demoralizing.

Because these young people are beginning the formal operations part of their lives, they can imagine a future very different from the present they now have. In the case of an ill young adolescent, he may well wonder if there will be any future to which he can look forward. Will he die before he graduates from high school? Or, if there is a future, what kind of future will it be? One with even more disabilities and limitations than he has at present?

These young people are also troubled by whether they will ever be "wanted" by someone romantically. Young people of this age are beginning the process of maturation of their sexual identities. Just at the time when they are being attracted to other persons romantically (or physically), they are experiencing a diminution in their own bodies. Perhaps they are not as manly or womanly as they hope. Perhaps they look chronically ill or much younger. These superficial aspects have very profound effects on their identities. Thus, these adolescents feel badly about themselves, feeling that they have very little to give of themselves. After all, who would want them when they could have an able-bodied person?

Preteens and young adolescents understand the notion that death is permanent. This causes them much distress, at least initially, because they must face death alone while all their friends and relatives will remain behind. In effect, they are being separated against their will, and they do not welcome it. Although they may come to accept their conditions as time goes on, the initial response is almost always anger and a sense of being cheated.

Spiritually, the preteen and young teen alternate between embracing the God of childhood and being angry at the God of the present. "Why am I sick and all my friends are well?" and "Am I being punished for something?" are common themes. No one wants to feel as if they are not in God's good graces, but when one is ill, one certainly wonders. An important difference between these young people and those younger is that they can ask some very pointed questions. They can also contemplate the future more keenly and are more affected by the thoughts of a future of incapacitation than is a younger child who is still under the daily care of a parent.

These adolescents' thoughts about God are obviously

affected by what they've been taught and what they've heard. But it is also based on their own reasoning powers. "What kind of God *lets* people be sick?" asked a thirteen-year-old girl with terminal cancer. "If I were God, I wouldn't even let anyone be sick. So, why does God let people be sick if God is smarter than all of us?" It is an answer that adults cannot give because we don't know any better than children and teens do. And, for young persons who know that their lives might be winding to a close, they wonder what kind of God they are going to and what kind of existence that they will experience. They mourn the loss of a long life, especially the long life that it appears all their friends will have. They mourn the death of many dreams. This mourning is even more acute as they become older.

# Pastoral Approaches

1. As children mature into young adolescents, their privacy and wishes must be respected, even more so than when they were younger. Many young adolescents welcome pastoral visitors, with or without their parents present. If a parent is present, ask the young person if she would prefer her parent to remain while you visit. Most young people of this age prefer their parents in the room when a stranger visits.

2. Some adolescents are turned off by their denomination and, by extension, anyone representing it. Still other adolescents may be angry at God for their illness and refuse to talk with anyone who might bring up the subject of God. So be sensitive. When visiting a young adolescent, greet him immediately when entering the

room and identify yourself. But, do not give the impression that you have only come to proselytize. One young teen who died of AIDS complained, "I don't want my pastor to visit me because he always seems like he's judging me or my mother because she did drugs and got AIDS and gave it to me. I hate it."

3. As with all patients, if the ill adolescent doesn't want to talk or even to have a visitor, don't remain. After all, you are there, as God's representative, for the benefit of a young sister or brother. You are not there for yourself. Even if your visit is very brief, as long as you respect the wishes of the young person, you might speak more about God's love for her than if you delivered an eloquent sermon. As an instrument of God, you never know how God will use you or what effect you may have on those you visit.

4. If the ill adolescent wishes to speak, let him lead the conversation. You might ask if there is anything that he would like to have. Do not force conversation about God or the church. If you do happen to bring it up, and the adolescent seems disinterested, let it go.

5. Many adolescents *will* bring up the subject of God and God's justice in letting people be ill or die. As with younger persons, answer questions as honestly and gently as possible. Demonstrate mercy and love, not sheer knowledge.

6. If the adolescent begins to cry, let him. If he apologizes for crying, reassure him that crying is a normal reaction to frustration, fear, or pain—all of which may be operant in his life at the moment. If the adolescent's tears disturb you, do *not* give that impression to the adolescent, and never say, "Don't cry." After all, your

discomfort is your problem and not that of the hurting adolescent. When an ill person is crying, ask if she would like a tissue or if she would like you to leave. Abide by the response that you receive. Above all, do not attempt to minimize the tears by making jokes or distracting the young person. Minimizing tears only trivializes them.

7. Keep in mind that an adolescent may be angry at God because of her illness. This is not always true, but it is a common reaction. Young adolescents may have been taught by their parents that God rewards goodness and punishes evil. When adolescents are seriously ill or injured, they, like younger children, wonder what they did that was so wrong to merit this degree of punishment. A pastoral visitor must be ready to hear some anger directed toward God without becoming defensive. Because God has given us all free will, God permits us to respond to both life and divine overtures freely. We can even reject God's gifts and love. In spite of this, God continues to love.

8. Thus, reassure the adolescent of God's love. Reassure him that God is present—even in the hospital or sickroom. If at all possible, encourage the young person to have some personal possession that reminds him of God and brings him comfort. Ask if there are favorite passages from Scripture that the adolescent would like to hear or read, and provide those.

9. Ask if the adolescent would like to pray, and abide by her response. If she declines the invitation, do not push the issue.

10. If she wishes to pray, ask her if she wants to lead the prayer. Again, abide by her wishes.

11. Before leaving, ask if you can return for another visit and if there is anything you can bring. Abide by the response you receive.

12. Ministry to parents continues to be important even when the ill child is an adolescent. Parents are parents, and parents of older children and teens need ministry as much (or more) than parents of younger children. The main difference between ministering to parents of younger children and parents of adolescents is that much of the ministry provided to the parents of older patients is done well away from the bedside of the child.

13. Parents of adolescents can be positively or negatively affected by what visitors say. Well-intentioned but ill-conceived statements can not only hurt a parent emotionally but also spiritually, especially if statements about God's judgment or will are included. It is important for the pastoral visitor to help mothers and fathers see what good parents they have been. This is best done through quiet conversation and encouragement, in effect bringing a distraught parent to a calmer level. Resist the temptation to give unsolicited advice. If your advice is sought, first find out what the parent is thinking. Above all, do not take sides when there are disagreements between the parents, between the parents and other relatives, or between the adolescent and family members.

14. There is no set formula on how to minister. Some parents respond well to quiet conversation; others do better by being held; still others prefer to simply have a supportive person silently in the room with them. Treat each situation as a unique event and each family as unique individuals.

15. Parents will wonder why this illness or this disease happened to this child. It is always best not to suggest rational human answers to issues that are non-rational. For example, who can say why one sibling has cystic fibrosis while the others are completely well? Who can say why one teen is paralyzed after a boating accident while the sibling accompanying him walked away with minor injuries? The important thing is to be present in the midst of the family's pain. Answers to such questions are not really expected, but the need to ask such questions (without fear of rejection) is paramount.

16. Parents should be asked if *they* want the visitor to pray with them (silently or aloud)—separately from the teen, if necessary; if they decline, respect that. In addition, parents should be given the option of leading the prayer themselves. Although many parents decline this invitation to lead prayer, others appreciate it and embrace it. Unless the visitor knows a particular parent well, a parent should *always* be asked his preference in these matters.

17. Before leaving, ask the parent if there is anything that you or your congregation can do. Don't assume that you know what any given parent needs; always ask. Some of what is needed might be practical (for example, doing some shopping for the family, looking after younger children), while other needed gifts might be more emotional in nature (for example, being able to call you when she just wants to talk). Certainly, all parents can benefit from prayers, but ask if they want their names published or spoken publicly at worship services. Some parents, especially in difficult times, need their privacy. Respect that. Also remember to ask if the other

parent or other children in the family need anything. Ask whether it would be okay for you to make a return visit. Always abide by the wishes of the family in each of these areas. Failure to keep a promise—especially with regard to a return visit—may be understood as rejection or a lack of concern, not only on the pastoral visitor's part but also on the part of God whose representative you are.

# CHAPTER 6

# Mid to Late Teens

*Piaget Stage: Formal Operations; Erikson Stage: Identity vs. Role Diffusion; Fowler Stage: Individuative-Reflective*

## Stages in Health

At this age, young people continue the process which began in early adolescence. They continue to meet persons with backgrounds quite different from that of their families and to encounter situations that they have never experienced. Some of these situations are morally challenging. In mid and late adolescence, there is even more independence and mobility than in younger years, so the absolute number of these new experiences and new acquaintances is increasing. New worlds are ever present. Older adolescents easily imagine themselves in novel situations or being someone other than themselves. They are making serious plans about what kind of adults they will be. Reasoning powers are at adult levels, even though their emotional responses are not consistently adult in character.

Older adolescents continue to separate themselves from

their parents, trying to forge their own identities. There still is the need, at least in some adolescents, to "try on" a variety of roles in order to discern who they really are. A common example of this is the adolescent's constant change of major in school or constant reevaluation of what he will do as his life's work. From the adolescent's perspective, it makes perfect sense to sample as many experiences (or as many friends) as possible; from the adult perspective, such behavior seems "scattered" or unfocused.

At the earlier stage, young adolescents ponder their religious traditions. At this older stage, adolescents turn inward, seriously pondering what *they themselves* believe. This takes a great deal of inner reflection, and it is certainly individual. No one can make a decision for mature persons about their beliefs. Even though an adolescent questions or criticizes her own faith tradition, it *is* still part of her past and therefore part of her, even if she refuse to attend any church services.

# Illness and Injury

Older adolescents think more and more like adults. On the one hand, they may think exactly like their parents; but on the other hand, they may be thinking independently, trying very hard to take stands opposite to those espoused by their parents. Their sense of independence is at a peak. They have jobs to earn spending money or tuition for school. They have learned to drive so that they can have freedom to go and come as they please. They are choosing their life goals and are using their time in school to prepare for those goals. They are learning about themselves sexually and may be sexually active. They are understanding themselves better and are beginning to think about what kind of life partner they would like to marry. They have had to make choices about sexual activity, alcohol or drug use, cheating in school, and so on. They have their own circle of friends whom their parents may or may not appreciate. In any of these developmental steps, young adults may make choices with which their parents would not agree; but in the task of separation from parents, it is important for young people to be able to decide for themselves, with guidance from adults whom they trust.

When young people of this age are ill, any or all of the above steps may be truncated or eliminated altogether. For example, because of illness, an adolescent might not be permitted to operate a motor vehicle alone or cannot have a job because he does not have the stamina or physical ability. Maybe he has missed so much time from school that he has lost interest in academics and has no aspirations for college attendance; maybe he doesn't even want to finish high school. Perhaps, the ill adolescent has few friends because people have rejected her or because illness keeps her at home. Because she might have had no opportunities to experiment with illicit behaviors (and cannot even imagine having the occasions to be able to do so), she might have never really been seriously tempted in these areas.

Older adolescents understand very clearly their limitations in comparison with others. They see what others can do and what they cannot do. They mourn what they have lost; they mourn for the future which is uncertain, especially if they have a terminal condition. At a time when everyone else is thinking about proms or college, these teens may be thinking about walking again or getting off oxygen. As their peers are separating from parents, these ill adolescents may need their parents' constant care or, in extreme cases, are smothered by parents who are afraid to let them do anything on their own for fear of harming their already precarious health.

If they do not have supportive friends of their own age, these young people run the risk of involuting and retreating into themselves. They expect that they will never be liked because they look or act differently. Their expectations of future friends or mates may be minimal. They may be sad and depressed over their lot, or they may act out, with almost a "what the heck" attitude. As one sixteen-year-old boy with HIV said to me, "What difference does it really make? After all, I'll probably be dead by the time I'm twenty, so I just have to do *everything* now. Who's going to stop me? When my folks say something to me, I just say, 'Yeah, you had *your* fun when you were out of school, but I'm not going to live that long.' So I gotta do what I gotta do now before it's too late." Acting out—sexually, with substances, or by illegal behaviors—is not always an aggressive act. Sometimes, it is an act of profound despair and hopelessness.

Older adolescents clearly understand that death is permanent. They see themselves as being robbed of a future. Although they may not believe in an afterlife, they certainly understand that what comes next will not be the same as what they now experience. For some, the next life is a nonentity; for others, it is negative in terms of its forced separation from those whom the adolescents hold dear; for still others, it has to be an improvement over the present existence.

Spiritually, these young people are usually very angry at the circumstances that cheated them out of a full life. They understand all too well what they are losing; they understand it far better than those much younger than them. Their mourning is intense for the life that they think should be theirs. Depending on their temperament, they may be weepy and depressed, angry and hostile, or risk-taking. A number of these young people give up belief in God because they are angry at God, and refuse to believe that a good God would permit them to be sick or die at a young age. "What kind of God lets kids, especially babies be sick?" asked a puzzled (and angry) fifteen-year-old. When they believe in God, they may express their anger in other ways, such as refusing to go to church, refusing to pray (or letting others pray for them), or refusing to speak with the pastor when he comes to visit. "Just go away and leave me alone," said a seventeen-year-old girl to her pastor when he came to visit. "I don't want to hear anything about God. All I want to hear from God is that I won't be sick anymore. Can you promise me that? If you can't, then get out!" Then she turned away and faced the wall.

# Pastoral Approaches

1. Respect the privacy and wishes of older adolescents. Most older adolescents welcome pastoral visitors, especially without their parents present. If parents are present, ask if the adolescent would prefer their presence while you visit. Abide by the response that is given to you.

2. Many older adolescents are turned off by their denomi-

nation and, by extension, anyone representing it. Still other adolescents may be angry at God for their illness and refuse to talk with anyone who might bring up the subject of God. So be sensitive. When visiting, greet the adolescent immediately when entering the room and identify yourself, but do not give the impression that you have only come to proselytize. One eighteen-year-old woman who died of AIDS complained, "I hope our deacon doesn't come to see me. He doesn't care about me; he only cares about whether he can preach at me. I'm too sick and tired to listen to him. He may be the church's deacon, but he's not *my* deacon."

3. As with all patients, if the ill adolescent doesn't want to talk or even to have a visitor, don't remain. After all, you are there, as God's representative, for the benefit of your younger sister or brother. You are not there for yourself. Even if your visit is very brief, as long as you respect the wishes of the young person, you might speak more about God's love for him than if you spoke the finest words. As an instrument of God, you never know how God will use you, or what effects you may have on those you visit.

4. If the ill adolescent wishes to speak, let her lead the conversation. You might ask if there is anything that she would like to have. Do not force conversation about God or the church. If you do happen to bring it up, and the adolescent seems disinterested, let it go.

5. Many adolescents will bring up the subject of God and God's justice in letting people be ill or die. They may want to debate with the pastoral visitor, trying to convince themselves that the visitor doesn't know as much as they do. As with younger persons, answer questions

as honestly and gently as possible. Demonstrate mercy, love, and forgiveness, even (and especially) when the adolescent has insulted you or your beliefs.

6. If the adolescent begins to cry, let him. Crying publicly is especially difficult for young men. If he apologizes for crying, provide reassurance that crying is a normal reaction to frustration, fear, or pain—all of which he may be experiencing. If the adolescent's tears disturb you, do *not* give that impression to the adolescent, and never say, "Don't cry." After all, your discomfort is your problem, and not that of the hurting adolescent. When an ill person is crying, either sit quietly or ask if he would like a tissue or if he would like you to leave. Abide by the response that you receive. Above all, do not attempt to minimize the tears by making jokes or distracting the person. This trivializes the pain.

7. Keep in mind that an adolescent may be angry at God because of her illness. This is not always true, but it is common. When many adolescents are seriously ill or injured, they, like younger children, wonder what they did that was so wrong to deserve the punishment of their current situation. A pastoral visitor must be ready to hear some anger directed toward God without becoming defensive. Because God has given us all free will, our God permits us to respond to both life and divine overtures freely. We can even reject God's gifts and love. In spite of this, God continues to love.

8. Thus, reassure the adolescent of God's love. Reassure her that God is present, even in the hospital or sickroom. If at all possible *and* if she is willing, encourage her to have some personal possession that brings her comfort. If the adolescent had indicated openness to

Scripture, ask if there are favorite passages that she would like to hear or read, and provide those.

9. Ask if the adolescent would like to pray, and abide by his response. If he declines the invitation, do not push the issue.

10. If he wishes to pray, ask him if he wants to lead the prayer. Again, abide by his wishes.

11. Before leaving, ask if you can return for another visit and if there is anything you can bring to him. Abide by the response you receive.

12. Ministry to parents continues to be important even when the ill child is an older adolescent. Parents are parents, and parents of older teens and young adults need ministry as much as (or more than) parents of younger children. The main difference between ministering to parents of younger children and parents of adolescents is that much of the ministry provided to the parents of older patients is done well away from the bedside of their child.

13. Parents of adolescents can be positively or negatively affected by what visitors say. Well-intentioned but ill-conceived statements can not only hurt a parent emotionally but also spiritually, especially if statements about God's judgment or will are included. It is important for the pastoral visitor to help mothers and fathers see what good parents they have been. This is best done through quiet conversation and encouragement, in effect bringing a distraught parent to a calmer, more rational level. As was true for the other age groups discussed in this book, do not give unsolicited advice to parents. If your advice is sought, first determine the parent's opinions or impressions. Above all, do not take

sides when there are disagreements between the parents, between the parents and other relatives, or between the adolescent and family members.

14. There is no set formula on how to minister. Some parents respond well to quiet conversation; others do better by being held; still others prefer to simply have a supportive person silently in the room with them. Treat each situation as a unique event and each family as unique individuals.

15. Parents will wonder why this illness or this disease happened to this child. It is always best not to suggest rational human answers to issues that are non-rational. For example, who can say why one sibling has cancer while the other is completely well? Who can say why one twin nearly died from an asthma attack while the other twin is entirely well? The important thing is to be present in the midst of the family's pain. Answers to such questions are not really expected, but the need to ask such questions is paramount.

16. Parents should be asked if they want the visitor to pray with them (silently or aloud)—separately from the teen, if necessary; if they decline, respect that. In addition, parents should be given the option of leading the prayer themselves. Although many parents decline this invitation to lead prayer, others appreciate it and embrace it. Unless the visitor knows a particular parent well, a parent should *always* be asked his preference in these matters.

17. Before leaving, ask the parent if there is anything that you or your congregation can do for her. Don't assume that you know what any given parent needs; always ask. Some of what is needed might be practical (for ex-

ample, running errands), while other needed gifts might be more emotional in nature (for example, being able to call you when she just wants to talk). Certainly, all parents can benefit from prayers, but ask if they want their names published or spoken publicly at worship services. Some parents, especially in difficult times, need their privacy. Respect that. Also remember to ask if the other parent or other children in the family need anything. Finally, ask if the parent would welcome a return visit, abiding by the response that is given. Always keep any promise that you make to the best of your ability. Failure to keep a promise—especially with regard to making a return visit—may be interpreted as rejection or lack of concern, not only on the part of the pastoral visitor but also on the part of God whose representative you are.

# PART TWO

# Special Considerations

# CHAPTER 7

# Chronic Illnesses

S ome children suffer from chronic illnesses that are fatal. Yet, the majority of children with chronic conditions do not have illnesses that are immediately fatal or terminal. Most of these children must learn to manage their lives affected, sometimes daily, by conditions for which there are no cures, but which are not life-threatening in the short run. These conditions run courses which are marked by times when they are quiescent (in remission) and times in which they flare-up (in exacerbation). These periods can be over the course of several weeks to months or, in the case of certain conditions, over the course of several hours (such as an asthmatic attack).

What are some of these conditions? Respiratory problems (such as asthma), gastrointestinal problems (such as colitis), genitourinary problems (such as kidney disease), glandular problems (such as diabetes or thyroid problems), skin conditions (such as eczema or psoriasis), central nervous system problems (such as seizures), connective tissue problems (such as arthritis or lupus), and blood disorders (such as hemophilia or sickle cell disease) are among the most common. With new therapies, even HIV infection is most properly thought of as a chronic condition than a rapidly terminal one.

Each of the conditions listed above (and the many others not listed) has its own set of signs and symptoms which mark flare-ups and remissions. Most of these signs and symptoms are well known to patients and their parents. Furthermore, many children and their families are fully aware of any events which may precipitate flare-ups and which conditions, therapies, or modalities promote resolution.

Insofar as a condition's flare can be predicted, those with chronic illnesses can feel somewhat in control of it and, consequently, of their lives. When a condition's flare cannot be predicted, a child or teen feels helpless, totally out of control, and at the mercy of the illness or condition. This means, practically speaking, that if a child cannot predict when she is likely to experience low blood sugar, she will feel as if she is walking on eggshells, never being quite comfortable with being away from home or away from parents, never being quite comfortable with her diet, or never being comfortable with her medications. This causes a great deal of anxiety, not only in the child or teen but also in her parents, who feel as if they cannot adequately protect their child unless they are with her constantly. Such parental overprotection, while understandable, does not promote maturation.

In addition, not all flares are equal. Some flare-ups of asthma, for example, require only extra doses of inhaled medications. Other flare-ups of the same disease require hospitalization and oxygen. Many children who have been doing very well with their chronic conditions experience a set-back when they incur a particularly serious flare, especially those requiring hospitalization. In addition to the normal amount of anxiety previously mentioned, serious flares precipitate an even greater level of anxiety as the child or teen wonders, "What if the next time is worse? What if they can't make me better next time? What if I die?" Parents, too, are concerned when the severity of flares is marked because it demonstrates how little control *they* themselves have.

Some chronic conditions are associated with mild flares. It is difficult to compare a flare-up of eczema with a worsening of a seizure disorder or diabetic ketoacidosis. Yet, for the person experiencing it, the flare-up of eczema may be seen as disfiguring and shameful while the flare-up of diabetes, while more serious, is invisible and thus may be regarded as less shameful. This is particularly true for adolescents for whom appearances are everything. To look different is to be different.

Chronic conditions are usually associated with the necessity of taking medications daily or undergoing certain therapies routinely. If these medications can be taken or these therapies undergone without the notice of friends or teachers, the affected child or teen generally has an easier time than if others must know about the medications or therapies. For example, if medication must be taken at school in the nurse's office and the child must leave class to take the medication, other students will notice and ask questions. If a child or teen must leave a class or leave school early to attend physical or occupational therapy, others will notice. This draws more attention not only to the student but also to his condition.

Similarly, increased attention is drawn to conditions which are either dramatic (for example, seizures) or badly misunderstood (for example, AIDS). The fear of such conditions leads to the likelihood of the affected person feeling even more alienated with the condition.

Whatever the condition, a chronic illness makes a child or teen feel different and forces him to consider his own mortality as he becomes older. A chronic condition is a constant, rude reminder that one's health status can change rather quickly. Naturally, this is true of most of us—through an injury or serious infection, any of us can lose our state of good health. The difference is that for persons with certain chronic conditions, this reality is ever present.

This can affect a person's trust in the future and trust in one's own body. For a child, it can also affect trust in parents who are incapable of protecting her from illness or disability. This lack of trust causes anxiety, fear, and sometimes a sense of doom and depression. Some children with chronic conditions consider suicide because they don't want to deal with the lack of predictability in their lives. They want to separate from parents, but fear that if they lose their parents they would be doomed. These fears lead to feelings of inadequacy and lowered self-esteem.

Some children test their chronic conditions by doing the things that they are not supposed to do just to see what will happen. Children who must watch their diets eat everything; children who must take certain medications fail to do so to see if they will become more ill. Other children become hyper-vigilant and become fearful of doing anything on their own. This, too, can lead to lowered self-esteem and feelings of inadequacy.

In terms of their future, children with chronic conditions wonder if they will ever marry or have children of their own. They wonder if they will die and how they will die. As morbid as it sounds, they wonder about the manner of their final moments.

Spiritually, many children with chronic conditions wonder why God lets them have such problems. When they are feeling well and their illnesses are in remission, they feel that they have God's favor; when they experience flare-ups, they feel that God is angry with them, punishing them, or trying to teach them a lesson. Many children bargain with God: "If you let me stay well, I'll always remember to say my prayers." This is fine as long as they are well. When they become ill, however, they become disheartened, believing that God is dissatisfied with them, or that they have somehow displeased God.

Children with chronic conditions may be particularly disheartened when they experience a worsening of their condition, or after a healing service, at which they earnestly prayed that their chronic condition be taken away. This is a natural reaction, but it is not a reason for children and teens not to attend healing services. However, it does point out that there must be preparation for their attendance, and there must be conversation as to what they expect will happen and when.

# Pastoral Approaches

1. For general information about the pastoral approaches to children of specific ages, see the appropriate chapters.
2. You may well be visiting children or teens during a period of worsening of their chronic conditions. Hence, these children and teens may be discouraged when you

visit. Keep your visit as upbeat as possible, but don't think that your role is to "cheer them up." Discouragement may be the most natural response to the flare-up of a chronic condition.

3. If at all possible, try to find out a little bit about a child's or teen's chronic condition before you visit. You might do this by reading a bit about it or by calling the parent and asking for some information. If your congregation has a parish nurse, she might be able to give you information. Knowing something about the condition the child or teen has may prevent you from asking the wrong questions or saying the wrong things.

4. Even if you or your children suffer from the same chronic condition as the child you are visiting, resist the temptation to say, "I know what you're going through" because *you* don't know what *this* child is going through. Instead, if the child or teen wants to talk, listen. Only if they ask whether you know what they mean should you volunteer the information, but keep it brief. After all, it is their time and illness, not yours.

5. If a child or teen is angry about the flare-up of their condition, do not judge their anger. Be with them, gently and lovingly, no matter what they say. We adults say things when we are ill or discouraged that we would not say when we are feeling better. Children and adolescents are no different. In addition, God is not afraid of honesty, as evidenced by the psalms (especially psalms 13, 22, 88, and 142), so why should we?

6. If a child or teen should wonder, "Why does God let this keep happening to me?" or "Why doesn't God just make me better forever?" do not give pat answers. In-

stead, emphasize that the flare-up is not God's judgment of her, and that God wants her to be as well as possible. Sometimes, children and teens will ask, "Why doesn't God give me a miracle and make me all better?" A good response to this is: "Miracles are wonderful, but they don't happen all the time. I understand why you want one. We don't know why miracles happen to certain people and not to others. But we do know that God helps people when they're sick by sending them people who will love them and take good care of them." Above all, emphasize that God loves them and always will.

7. If a child or teen expresses, "I'm so sick of being like this; I wish I were dead," take the comment seriously. A number of children and teens with chronic conditions contemplate suicide because they "can't take it anymore" or because "no one will listen to me."

8. Pray with the child or teen if he wishes, but do not insist on it. Allow him to voice his own prayers, if he wishes, and do not "clean up" the prayers if they do not sound like the prayers adults would say.

9. Ask if it is all right if you come and see the child or teen again. If he agrees to a return visit, make sure you make the visit. Failure to do so may be construed as rejection. Failure of a pastoral visitor to return may also be interpreted as rejection on God's part (since you are representing God) or confirmation that a flare-up in her chronic condition is punishment from God.

10. Remember to minister to the child's or teen's parents. It is a huge responsibility to have a child with a chronic condition that can't be cured. Show your support. Offer to pray with them, but always ask first if they want

to take the lead. Ask if there is anything that you or members of the congregation can do to assist them and their family. You may need to ask more than once. Make sure that you follow through on any promises that you make (especially if you promise to make a return visit). Offer proof of God's love for them, not only in words but, more importantly, in actions.

11. Don't forget the siblings of the ill child. It is very hard to be a child or teen in a family in which one's sibling receives all the attention. Siblings suffer, too, when a brother or sister is ill, so overtures should be made to them as well. Parents can provide suggestions as to what you or other members of your congregation (especially children) can do for the siblings. *Always* follow through on any promises that you make, especially with regard to making return visits to minimize the chance that a family might feel abandoned by their church when they most need assistance.

# CHAPTER 8

# Mental Illnesses

I n our society, mental illnesses have a stigma that most physical conditions do not have. This is true even for children and teens with these conditions. Somehow, even though millions of people have mental illnesses, a prevailing attitude is that affected people should just "get their act together" and that they could help themselves if they tried. In truth, this is nonsense.

What kinds of diagnoses are subsumed under mental illnesses? Entities such as depression, obsessive-compulsive disorder, scrupulosity, autism, schizophrenia, antisocial behavior, and oppositional behaviors are included, but naturally there are many others. Some conditions are better understood than others. Some are more frightening than others (such as paranoid schizophrenia, in which a person hears voices telling him to do something wrong, or autism in which a person seems to be totally in a world of his own without regard for anyone or anything else). On the other hand, some seem, at least on the surface, even manageable or more harmless.

Because there is less sympathy for many mental illnesses than there are for most physical illnesses, the person (and her family) is less likely to find needed support. Instead they might find frank fear, loathing, or avoidance. Unfortunately, because of a serious lack of understanding of the causes, courses, and therapies for most mental illnesses, many people do not think of them as "illnesses." Yet, as much as children and teens with physical conditions need to experience God's love, so too (and perhaps even more so) do children and teens with mental illnesses need to experience this love and the sure knowledge that they also are valued children of God.

Many mental illnesses are associated with normal physical states, although in some (if not all) mental illnesses, there are certainly abnormalities in certain brain chemicals. This means that many persons with mental illness look normal but may not act normally. Because human beings are so wedded to appearances, it is not surprising that the mental illnesses of these persons are not fully appreciated. Medications may (and usually do) alter brain chemistry, but usually do not affect the way a person looks. Thus, mental illness may be invisible.

Taking medications chronically affects children and teens in different ways. Some may welcome their medications as their key to feeling better. For others, the need for daily medication is another rude reminder that they are not normal ("My brain's not even normal!" cried one ten-year-old), and that it takes chemicals to make them normal. Having to take medications every day *is* a bother. Such children may blame their parents for their conditions or may blame the doctors who prescribe the medications (especially if the medications have adverse side effects which the child or teen hates). "All I want to be is like everyone else," said a depressed child.

To take depression as an example, some children with depression have a strong family history of depression in other family members of different generations; there may even be a history of suicides. Other children and teens seem to experience depression because of what has happened to them (such as abuse, the death—especially traumatic—of parents or siblings, the effects of war, and so on). In other children and teens, it is difficult to know what has caused the depression. Depression can lead to a serious lowering of self-esteem and a sense of worthlessness; suicidal thoughts may intrude.

Spiritually, the depressed child or teen may not be able to access God, no matter how hard she tries and no matter what methods are used to assist her to do so. She may be unsure of whether God exists or, as we have seen in other chapters, why God lets her suffer. "Why didn't God stop that man from hurting me, and why won't God talk to me now? Doesn't God like me?" asked a bewildered six-year-old girl. "If God won't talk to me, then I won't talk to God," reasoned an eight-year-old. "After all, what's God done for me lately?"

There is the likelihood that a pastoral visitor will be seeing a child or teen precisely at the time that his mental illness has required acute intervention, such as a hospitalization. Hospitalizations for mental illness sometimes bring relief because it means that help is available. For other persons, it is concrete proof that they are defective mentally. This is especially true if the young person is being hospitalized for a suicide attempt. Although some may see suicide as a supremely selfish act, for many children and teens who attempt suicide, they see it as the only way out of a life that is no longer worth living. It is all too much for them to bear, and no one seems to be able to really help them. In their minds, this is even true of God.

# Pastoral Approaches

1. For general information about the pastoral approaches to children of specific ages, see the appropriate chapters.
2. If at all possible, try to find out a little bit about a child's or teen's mental illness before you visit. You might do this by reading a bit about it or by calling the parent and asking for some information. If your congregation has a parish nurse, she might be able to give you information. Knowing something about the condition the child or teen has may prevent you from asking the wrong questions or saying the wrong things.
3. For children and teens who are aware of their mental problems, they frequently experience a diminution of their self-esteem. Many times, they think that they are really defective. Remember the child who wailed, "My brain's not even normal!" Reassure them that they are loved by God just as they are.
4. Some children and teens with mental illnesses might behave in ways that are frightening. Do not act fearful of them because that might cause them to act even more frightening in order to get a further reaction from you. Alternatively, they might retreat from you. As a representative of God, your job is to manifest God's love. When in doubt, try to imagine how Jesus would treat them and act accordingly.
5. If a child or teen expresses, "I'm so sick of being like

this; I wish I were dead," take the comment seriously. A number of children and teens with mental conditions contemplate suicide because they "can't take it anymore." This is especially true of depression and paranoid schizophrenia.

6. Pray with the child or teen if she wishes, but do not insist on it. Allow her to voice her own prayers, if she wants, but don't try to "clean up" prayers that don't sound like proper prayers. In our anguish, God hears our honesty. Do likewise.

7. Ask if it is all right if you come and see the child or teen again. If he agrees to a return visit, make sure you do so. Failure to do so may be construed as rejection. Failure of a pastoral visitor to return may also be construed as rejection by God (since you are God's representative) or confirmation that mental illness is shameful.

8. Remember to minister to the child's or teen's parents. It is a huge responsibility to have a child with a mental illness, especially because they receive so little sympathy. Show your support and God's love. Offer to pray with them, but always allow them to take the lead. Ask if there is anything that you or members of the congregation can do to assist them and their family. You may need to ask more than once. Make sure that you follow through on any promises that you make, especially a promise to make a return visit. Offer proof of God's love for them, not only in words but, more importantly, in actions.

9. Don't forget the siblings of the mentally ill child. It is very hard to be a child or teen in a family in which one's sibling receives all the attention. Siblings suffer, too, when a brother or sister has a mental illness, espe-

cially when the illness has negative overtones. So, overtures should be made to them as well. Parents can provide suggestions as to what you or other members of your congregation (especially children) can do for the siblings. *Always* follow through on any promises that you make to decrease the likelihood that family members will feel abandoned by their church in their time of greatest need.

CHAPTER 9

# Catastrophic Injuries

When a child or teen incurs a serious or life-threatening injury, many questions are asked. "Why did this happen? Could it have been prevented? Whose fault was it?" Older children and teens may ask themselves these questions, but parents of any age child invariably ask these questions, seeking reassurance that the injury was not *their* own failure to adequately protect their child.

Injuries in an otherwise normal child turns a parent's world upside down immediately. When he left for school in the morning, the ten-year-old was completely healthy; by nightfall, he is comatose and on life-support systems. When a child or teen has a chronic or terminal condition, a parent has time to adjust to a diminution of physical abilities; this is true of the child or teen as well. In a traumatic injury, there is no time to prepare or to adjust. One minute, the child or teen is well, and the next minute, she is incapacitated.

Traumatic injuries vary in their severity and in their aftereffects. The most common and serious traumatic injuries are those caused by drowning or diving accidents,

those caused by motor vehicle accidents (either as a pas-
senger or pedestrian), those caused by burns (such as house
fires), and those caused by violent trauma (such as gunshot
wounds, knife wounds, or blunt trauma). Also included in
this category of violent trauma would be physical abuse
and rapes. All of these injuries can range from fatal to minor. Any of these injuries can cause paralysis (depending
on the degree and site of injury). Depending on the loca-
tion of blunt trauma, there may be abdominal, chest, head,
or spinal cord injury. Some of these injuries require immediate surgery while others do not. Some require months of
rehabilitation while others lend themselves to a more rapid
resolution and return to the child's or teen's previous state
of physical health.

The shock of being well and then finding oneself in
traction, on a respirator, or paralyzed cannot be described.
Naturally, disbelief and depression are likely. This is true
of all but the youngest of children who do not fully understand the seriousness of their injuries. For older children
and teens, they understand only too well what they could
once do (maybe even just a day or two before) and what
they can no longer do. They are understandably frightened and panicky. If the child or teen has a clear recollec-
tion of the trauma, this heightens her psychic discomfort
as she relives the trauma. This is also true of parents who
were present when the trauma occurred.

Most children and teens in this situation believe that
they will get better, and it is important for them to hold
this belief, since it can spur them on when they become
discouraged. Of course, many of these injuries *do* get better. Broken bones knit together; burns heal; lacerations are
replaced by new tissue. However, even when healing will

occur, it may be accompanied by much pain and numerous procedures and therapies. This may take much more time than most children or teens expect because they still think of themselves as they were before the accident.

In other cases, complete recovery is not possible. Severed spinal cords do not return to wholeness; gunshot wounds to the head may permanently impair a child or teen's ability to speak or move; and, although therapy may well improve a child's or teen's initial condition, it might not return him to the state of health he previously enjoyed. This can cause the child or teen enormous frustration and sadness (if she is aware of her deficits) and certain agony for the parents and siblings.

Many children and teens who have experienced traumatic injuries have recurring "flashbacks" of the events leading up to the injury and sometimes the injury itself. The child who nearly drowned has recurrent nightmares about his inability to breathe in the water. The teen who was shot in a hold-up attempt has intruding thoughts of seeing his assailant and hearing the gunshots, over and over. The child who was burned in a house fire reports that she can't stop smelling the odor of her burning flesh, even months later. The teen who was injured in a motor vehicle accident panics every time she sees a van that looks like the one that hit her car. These flashbacks are not necessarily proportional to the severity of the injury, because sometimes persons with rather minor injuries have the most vivid flashbacks, while others who were more seriously injured remember nothing at all of the episodes.

Parents' sense of the future for their child or teen becomes completely overturned after a traumatic injury. In the case of catastrophic injury, parents worry about their child's future abilities, including job possibilities. They are also concerned about who will care for her if something happens to them. Aware older children and teens share this same concern. Parental concerns about the cost of needed therapy might also be great, especially if the family lacks adequate health insurance. Anger at themselves for not better supervising their child, anger at their child for sustaining the injury (as illogical as that sounds), anger at those who perpetrated or caused the injury, and anger at each other for various reasons can be expected. Many marriages suffer enormously when catastrophic injuries occur to family members. Because of anger at each other, overwhelming fatigue, and decreased self-esteem, a couple's emotional and sexual relationship may suffer. Some marriages cannot bear the strain and end in divorce.

Many parents may feel that they are too busy to pray or to go to church because they have to attend to their child's or teen's needs. Others may be angry at God for not preventing the injury ("Why didn't God protect my son from that cross fire?" "Why did God let my daughter hit her head?" "Why didn't God make it rain so that the kids couldn't have gone swimming?") or angry at God for not providing a miraculous recovery. ("God heals other people; why not my kid?") Parents may be angry at pastoral visitors (lay or ordained) since they are representatives of God. Other parents are not angry at God, but feel as if God has left them completely alone and does not hear their pleas for help.

# Pastoral Approaches

1. For general information about the pastoral approaches to children of specific ages, see the appropriate chapters.

2. If at all possible, try to find out a little bit about a child's or teen's injury and condition before you visit. This is to better prepare you for the sights and odors you might encounter, and to help you avoid looking shocked when you first enter the child's or teen's room. Knowing something about the extent of the injuries may prevent you from asking the wrong questions or saying the wrong things.

3. For children and teens who are aware of their injuries, they may be feeling very depressed as they think about their present condition. Be prepared for that. Be positive without expecting that you are going to "cheer them up." After all, a degree of depression might be the most appropriate reaction to their injuries.

4. Some children and teens with severe injuries look frightening because of all the medical equipment hooked up to them. Do not let your fear or apprehension be revealed in your voice or actions. Do not act fearful because they might retreat emotionally from you. Do not act shocked because they might interpret that as proof that they are in a worse condition than they really are. As a representative of God, your job is to manifest God's love. When in doubt, try to imagine how Jesus would treat them and act accordingly. If you truly feel that you will "lose it" if you visit, get a replacement for yourself.

5. If a child or teen expresses, "I'm so sick of being like this; I wish I were dead," take the comment seriously. A number of children and teens with severe, irreversible injuries contemplate suicide because they "can't take it anymore." This is especially true when children or teens become paralyzed or when their appearance has changed drastically because of the injury.

6. Be especially sensitive if the child's or teen's injury was caused by physical abuse, sexual abuse, or rape. Some children and teens suffering from any of these feel "dirty." By your words and your actions, clearly give the message that they are loved by God. Because the child or teen might not want you to know that she was raped (for example), don't bring the subject up unless she does. If she does, gently, but firmly, relay the message that the rape (or abuse) was *not* her fault.

7. Pray with the child or teen if she wishes, but do not insist on it. Allow her to voice her own prayers, if she wishes. Do not be surprised if the prayers are full of anger—at the perpetrator or at God. One child prayed, "Why did you let this happen to me?" banging her fists against her pillow. Such a prayer shows that she still has a relationship with God. True, she doesn't understand why God, who could have protected her, did not; yet she is still able to communicate her frustration, sadness, and disappointment to God.

8. Ask if it is okay if you come and see the child or teen again. If he agrees to a return visit, make sure you do so. Failure of a pastoral visitor to return may be interpreted as rejection by God (since you are God's representative) or confirmation that the young person's appearance is off-putting.

9. Remember to minister to the child's or teen's parent. It is an enormous responsibility to have a child with a catastrophic injury. Show your support and God's love. Remember, the parents are hurting, too. Offer to pray with them, but always allow them to take the lead. Ask if there is anything that you or members of the congregation can do to assist them and their family. You may need to ask more than once. Make sure that you follow through on any promises that you make. Offer proof of God's love for them, not only in words but, more importantly, in actions.

10. Don't forget the siblings of the injured child. It is very hard to be a child or teen in a family in which one's sibling receives all the attention. Siblings suffer too when a brother or sister has faced major trauma, especially when the circumstances of the trauma have negative overtones. Thus, overtures should be made to them as well. Parents can provide suggestions as to what you or other members of your congregation (especially children) can do for the siblings. *Always* follow through on any promises that you make.

# CHAPTER 10

# Terminal Illnesses

Children and teens with terminal illnesses are in a special category. Although any condition that we have discussed could be terminal because of serious flare-ups, in this chapter, we will deal with two of the most common terminal illnesses of children and teens today—cancer and AIDS.

There are as many different types of cancers as there are cell types in the body. Although we know what causes certain cancers, we do not know what causes others. Furthermore, even when we know what causes certain cancers, that does not mean that we can predict completely who will develop a malignancy. For example, we know that smoking is associated with lung cancer. Yet, not every person who smokes gets lung cancer, and some people get lung cancer who have never smoked. As another example, many people who were exposed to the nuclear blast in Hiroshima over fifty years ago died of cancer. But not all did.

Cancer is a deranged, uncontrolled proliferation of cells. The usual bodily mechanisms to limit cell growth do not work. The immune system, which normally acts as a surveillance system and detects abnormal cells when they are few in number, has not done its job for reasons that are not clear. Thus, a few abnormal cells are permitted to multiply and grow in number, creating a tumor.

In the case of AIDS, this condition is generally thought of as the terminal phase of an HIV infection. HIV is a virus, which attacks certain white blood cells called lymphocytes. Lymphocytes are necessary for our health because they help us fight certain infections. The HIV virus inserts itself inside the nucleus of the lymphocyte cell, thus ensuring that it will make more copies of itself. The virus causes multiple organ disease and failure. Persons with AIDS generally waste away and die of overwhelming infections, respiratory failure, kidney failure, or heart failure. HIV can also attack the brain and central nervous system. *No* organ system is immune from its effects.

Children and teens experience certain malignancies that older persons do not and vice versa. Likewise, children and teens experience different manifestations of HIV infection than do older persons and vice versa.

Many malignancies are curable, although the therapy required to do this is likely to be prolonged, unpleasant, and painful. As of this writing (2002), HIV infection can be controlled (but not cured) by taking many, many medications each day.

This chapter's focus is on the terminal stages of both of these diseases. In both cases, parents probably have been told the prognosis. In the case of HIV, the parent(s) may already be deceased from the same disease, so the caretaker of the infected child or teen may be a grandparent, other relative, or foster parent. In both situations, parents and other caretakers struggle with whether to tell the child or teen of his diagnosis and prognosis. Will telling him prompt him to take medications or adhere to therapy more closely? Or will it depress or demoralize him (potentially leading to a more rapid loss of health)? Will telling her make her consider suicide? Will telling her deprive her of happy days without worry or does it, instead, give her an opportunity to bring closure to her life?

It has been my experience that many elementary-school children and teens know how ill they are without anyone telling them. As one child said to me, "Don't tell my mom and dad, but I don't think I'm gonna get out of the hospital. They keep telling me what a big birthday party I'm gonna have in our yard, but it's not gonna happen." In an effort to protect their parents or caretakers, children and teens do not reveal their insights, fears, or hopes.

Initially, when they learn that they are so ill, children and teens go through stages similar to those described by Elisabeth Kubler-Ross in adults. Not all children and teens go through the stages exactly as she described them, but knowing the stages helps caregivers and pastoral visitors to better understand where a child or teen is in his or her understanding.

The first stage is *denial*: the diagnosis is wrong, the doctors are stupid. The second stage is *anger*: if only the doctors had run the correct test, I wouldn't be dying now. If only I had eaten vegetables, I wouldn't have cancer now. If only I had different parents, I wouldn't have AIDS. The third stage is *bargaining*: if I promise to say my prayers every day and never hit my brother again, God will make me okay again. The fourth stage is *sadness*: God isn't helping me and I'm not getting better; I guess that there is nothing that can help me now. The final stage is *acceptance*.

These stages do not have to be experienced in the order given, and anyone can experience a stage more than once. This is especially true if a remission occurs, and a child or teen has convinced himself that he is going to get better permanently only to become seriously ill several months later. As we have seen before, it is the unpredictability of illness that is the most difficult aspect for many children, teens, and adults to bear.

If the pastoral visitor is seeing a child or teen soon after she has been told that she is very ill with cancer or AIDS, and if this child or teen really had not suspected the diagnosis, special care must be given. Children and teens who are dying can be weepy and depressed, or angry and depressed. They can say hateful, hurtful things while, at the same time, wanting to be held. They can make plans to give away their personal belongings at the same time they are clutching them tightly. Sometimes, the most supportive thing a pastoral visitor can do is to sit silently in solidarity with such a child or teen, not attempting to lead the conversation, but allowing the young person to take the lead. This is very hard, because we adults want to "make it better." But we can't. Chattering on might be more for *our* benefit than for the one at whose bedside we sit.

In the case of children and teens dying with AIDS, they frequently do not even have the comfort of being able to be open and honest about their condition because of the lingering societal stigma against persons with that disease. Even though these children and teens did nothing themselves to contract the disease, it is still more difficult emotionally to be dying from AIDS than from other diseases. In addition, they may be embarrassed for a pastoral visitor to know that they have AIDS, thinking that such a person might also reject them as others have.

Spiritually, these children and teens have serious questions about God's motives in permitting them to be so ill. This is especially true for children and teens who contracted HIV from their mothers. "Just because my mother did drugs, why do I have to die?" cried a ten-year-old girl. Some children and teens may even believe that God is *making* them ill on purpose to teach them a lesson. In either event, they may not want to pray, hear about God, or see anyone from the church.

# Pastoral Approaches

1. For general information about the pastoral approaches to children of specific ages, see the appropriate chapters.
2. If at all possible, try to find out a little bit about a child's or teen's condition before you visit. This is to better prepare you for the sights and odors you might encounter, and to help you avoid looking shocked when you first enter the child's or teen's room. Knowing something about the condition may prevent you from asking the wrong questions or saying the wrong things.
3. Children and teens who are aware of their diagnosis and prognosis may be feeling very depressed as they think about their present condition and their future. Be prepared for that. Be positive without expecting that you are going to "cheer them up." After all, a degree of depression might be the most appropriate reaction to the thought of dying at a young age. Your job is to be a manifestation of God's love for and presence to them.
4. Some children and teens who are dying look frighten-

ing because of all the medical equipment hooked up to them. Do not let your fear or apprehension be revealed in your voice or actions. Do not act fearful because they might retreat emotionally from you. Do not look shocked because they might conclude that they are closer to the end of their lives than they really are. As a representative of God, your job is to manifest God's love. When in doubt, try to imagine how Jesus would treat them and act accordingly. If you really think that you might "lose it" if you visit, find another pastoral visitor to make the visit.

5. If a child or teen expresses, "I'm so sick of being like this; I wish I were dead," take the comment seriously. A number of children and teens with severe, irreversible illnesses, such as cancer or AIDS, contemplate suicide because they "can't take it anymore." Let such young people know that you and their congregation pray for their healing.

6. If you make more than one visit, do not be surprised if a child's or teen's vitality diminishes with each visit. The work of dying saps one's energy. At some visits, he may be less willing to communicate than at other visits. Respect that. All you need to do is be present; God will do the rest.

7. Pray with the child or teen if he wishes, but do not insist on it. Allow him to voice his own prayers, if he wishes. Do not be surprised if the prayers are full of anger—at "whoever" caused the illness or at God.

8. Ask if it is okay if you come and see the child or teen again. If she agrees to a return visit, make sure you do so. Failure to do so may be interpreted as rejection. Failure of a pastoral visitor to return may also be inter-

preted as rejection by God (since you are God's representative). This is especially true in the case of AIDS because of the stigma that is associated with it. But a perception of rejection by God is particularly damaging and traumatic when anyone (child, teen, or adult) is facing death from any cause.

9. Remember to minister to the child's or teen's parent. It is an overwhelming responsibility and tragedy to have a child who is dying. It seems so unnatural. Many parents feel as if they are "going out of our minds." Show your support and God's love. Remember, they are hurting immensely. Offer to pray with them, but always allow them to take the lead. Ask if there is anything that you or members of the congregation can do to assist them and their family. You may need to ask more than once. Abide by any responses that are given, but keep in mind that responses may change over time. Make sure that you follow through on any promises that you make, especially those with regard to return visits or calls. Offer proof of God's love for them, not only in words but, more importantly, in actions.

10. Don't forget the siblings of the ill child. It is very hard to be a child or teen in a family in which one's sibling receives all the attention. Siblings suffer, too, when a brother or sister has a terminal illness, especially when the illness has negative overtones. After all, they are grieving also. Thus, overtures should be made to them as well. Parents can provide suggestions as to what you or other members of your congregation (especially children or teens) can do for the siblings.

11. When the child or teen has died, make sure to call or visit the family and offer to assist with any arrange-

ments or services that the parents are considering. Remember the siblings as well, because they too need much support, and their parents might not be in any position to provide it.

12. Try to keep in contact with the family for at least a year after the death. Parents have said that they received much support at the time of the death, but much less (even as little as two to three weeks) after the death. Again, remember the siblings in your contacts with the family. If the siblings attend a church school, make sure that their teachers are aware of their loss and how they are coping with that loss at home, at school, or in the neighborhood.

CHAPTER 11

# Conclusion

## The Impact
## of Dying Children and Their Families
## on the Church and Society

As much as we hate to hear of dying children, especially those in our midst, children and teens *are* dying daily, even in a country as privileged as our own. In other, poorer countries, the situation is much worse.

For too long, the Church has failed to train its seminarians and pastoral visitors in ministry to children and their families. There are a number of reasons for this. First, it *is* difficult ministry. Second, there are not many qualified persons to do the training well. Third, there is the hope that dying children and teens represent a very small group and that most congregations will never encounter the situation. Fourth, at times it seems that the Church has adopted society's attitude that raising and caring for one's children is a private affair, not a communal one.

Although many congregations will not have the experience of having a dying child in its midst, every congregation will have the experience of having an ill child or teen in its midst. This is reality.

That said, if we only care about ill and dying children belonging to our own congregations, we miss the boat. There are many children and teens, some of whom who are unchurched, who are not part of our immediate group but who are still our sisters and brothers, members of the Body of Christ. That is why the fourth reason listed above— that raising and caring for children is a private affair only— cannot be seriously embraced in a Christian congregation.

Naturally, parents have the right to raise children as they see fit, morally and ethically, but they can always use support from those around them. No time highlights this situation more clearly than at the time of illness. In addition, there are many children and teens whose parents are absent (physically, emotionally, or spiritually); what becomes of them when they are ill? We, as the Church, need to be the beacon for society, an example of how to treat children and teens, even those who don't belong to "us," because they belong to God, and indeed that is all that matters.

In the end, it really all comes down to Matthew 25.

> Then the king will say to those at his right hand, "…I was hungry and you gave me food, I was thirsty and you gave me something to drink, I was a stranger and you welcomed me, I was naked and you gave me clothing, I was sick and you took care of me, I was in prison and you visited me." Then the righteous will answer him, "Lord, when was it that we saw you hungry and gave you food, or thirsty and gave you something to drink? And when

was it that we saw you a stranger and welcomed you, or naked and gave you clothing? And when was it that we saw you sick or in prison and visited you?" And the king will answer them, "Truly I tell you, just as you did it to one of the least of these who are members of my family, you did it to me" (25:34–40).

# Bibliography

Alexander, Debra Whiting. *Children Changed by Trauma: A Healing Guide.* (Oakland, Calif.: New Harbinger Publications), 1999.

Bluebond-Langner, Myra. *In the Shadow of Illness: Parents and Siblings of the Chronically Ill Child.* (Princeton, N.J.: Princeton University Press), 2000.

Fitzgerald, Helen, and Elisabeth Kubler-Ross. *The Grieving Child: A Parent's Guide.* (New York: Simon & Schuster), 1992.

Fitzgerald, Helen. *The Grieving Teen: A Guide for Teenagers and Their Friends.* (New York: Turtleback), 2000.

Fowler, James. *Stages of Faith: The Psychhology of Human Development.* (San Francisco: HarperSanFrancisco), 1995. (He also does a great job of explaining Piaget and Erikson.)

Huntley, Theresa. *Helping Children Grieve When Someone They Love Dies.* (Minneapolis: Augsburg Fortress), 2002.

Keene, Nancy, and Rachel Prentice. *Your Child in the Hospital: A Practical Guide for Parents.* (Sebastopol, Calif.: O'Reilly & Associates), 1999.

Komp, Diane. *A Window to Heaven.* (Grand Rapids: Zondervan), 1992.

Komp, Diane. *A Child Shall Lead Them.* (New York: Steeple Hill), 1993.

Kubler-Ross, Elisabeth, MD. *On Children and Death: How Children and Their Parents Can and Do Cope With Death.* (New York: Simon & Schuster), 1997.

Parachin, Victor. *How to Comfort the Grieving: A Dozen Ways to Say "I Care"* (pamphlet) (Liguori, Mo.: Liguori Publications), 1991.

# About the Author

D r. Pat Fosarelli holds a doctorate in medicine from the University of Maryland School of Medicine and a doctorate in ministry from Wesley Theological Seminary. She is currently the Pastoral Associate of Corpus Christi Church in downtown Baltimore. In addition, she serves on the part-time faculty of the Johns Hopkins School of Medicine (Department of Pediatrics) and the faculty (Spirituality and Practical Theology) of the Ecumenical Institute of Theology, both in Baltimore.